D1271616

CRUS CLASSÉS DE GRAVES

THE HEART OF BORDEAUX

THE GREATEST WINES FROM GRAVES CHÂTEAUX

CRUS CLASSÉS DE GRAVES

THE HEART OF BORDEAUX

THE GREATEST WINES FROM GRAVES CHÂTEAUX

Preface by HUGH JOHNSON
Introduction by MICHEL BETTANE
Text by JAMES LAWTHER
Photographs by ALAIN BENOIT

Stewart, Tabori & Chang
New York

To past generations of winemakers, servants of our terroirs, who have followed each other for centuries… and to those of tomorrow so that they may continue to give us through their great wines this subtle mixture of mystery and excellence. And to you, who, through your passion for wine, convey a philosophy, a knowledge and a love of life.

Véronique Sanders-van Beek
President of the Union des Crus Classés de Graves

Contents

The World Atlas of Wine by Hugh Johnson and Jancis Robinson, 6th edition, Mitchell Beazley, London, 2007.

Preface

Hugh Johnson

My fellow countrymen have had a fondness for what we call claret for many centuries; eight, at least, and if Roman records can be believed, perhaps even 19 or 20. In the Middle Ages it was our national drink. We were then largely deprived of it until the 17th century, when it made a dramatic reappearance in London in a revolutionary guise.

It is the best-known story in England's drinking history. The London diarist Samuel Pepys, who recorded his daily doings with a frankness permitted him by his coded language, went to the city's most fashionable tavern and "drank a sort of French wine, called Ho Bryan that hath a good and most particular taste that I ever met with." In that one word "particular" he defined a revolution—and initiated a literature of tasting notes that has since become a flood.

Tasting notes from further back in history rarely give us any hint that wines had recognizable features, anything you would call "particularities." I have a few favorites. The best is Shakespeare's "marvellous searching wine, and it perfumes the blood e'er one can say 'What's this?'" Does Michelangelo's description of a wine that "kisses, licks, bites, thrusts and stings" bring any particular wine to mind? I suspect a late-harvested one, at least.

The Haut-Brion that inspired Pepys's comment was claret with attitude. He expected Bordeaux to offer fresh, sapid, lightly tannic and mildly acidic red wine, pale in color. What he drank that night had more color, more body, more concentration and depth, perhaps the scent of new oak, but above all a sense of place. It was an original, with a character he had never met before. And customers were ready to pay whatever it cost.

The fashion caught on instantly. England, with the restoration of its "merry monarch," Charles II, was open to new notions of luxury. When the curious investigated further, though, they were puzzled. The philosopher John Locke visited Haut-Brion and reported "nothing but pure white sand, mixed with a little gravel. One would imagine it scarce fit to bear anything." Welcome to Pessac-Léognan.

Particularity is the hallmark of Bordeaux's *Crus Classés*. In a region awash with wine of all sorts they stand out as *marques* that maintain certain attributes year after year—even century after century. Sand and gravel, and what lies under them, set the parameters. The floods of the Garonne over millennia have deposited this variable layer of easily shifted shingle over already variable limestone and clay.

Vines once planted in desperation, as a subsistence crop where nothing else could grow, found singular flavors in these gravel beds. Proprietors preferred one vine or another, experimented and honed their own favorite selections. Over time a certain recipe, as it were, applied to a certain parcel of land, gave a consistent and distinct result: a cru with a life, both economic and gastronomic, of its own.

A score of such individual enterprises make up the whole body of *Crus Classés* of Graves. They are scattered over a surprisingly wide area, 12 kilometers by 7 or 8, and interrupted by woods and villages, highways and suburbs, because the formula only works where the accumulated soil has reached a depth, and created an exposition facing the sun, susceptible to ripening grapes. Red or white grapes, be it noted: this is a versatile formula, with experience proving that on certain sites the classic Bordeaux recipe of Sauvignon Blanc and Sémillon in varying, personal-to-the-property, proportions can conjure up white wines as complex and long-lived as the region's reds (and as the best of Burgundy).

How to sum up the qualities of a region whose wines can create emotion without drama, and take you to the very heart of the claret conundrum? It was an Edwardian Irish solicitor, Maurice Healy by name, who ventured to identify the style of claret from the soils of the Graves, of which Pessac-Léognan is the heart, by contrasting it with the Médoc.

Graves and Médoc wines, he said, are like matt and glossy prints of the same photograph. Like Pepys's "particular," his remark focuses comprehension. You are at liberty, of course, to prefer one or the other. Would you say the matt print has more *sérieux*, draws you in to look deeper, satisfies you with subtler shadings than the light-reflecting gloss?

In the essay that follows Michel Bettane goes as far as language can in evoking savors that only the nose and mouth can perceive, and the brain enjoy. It is the glory of France to have created such gustatory works of art, the happy fate of Pessac-Léognan to provide the milieu, and the pride and joy of their guardians and curators to polish the jewels in the keeping.

Introduction

Michel Bettane

Wines from Graves were my first initiation into the joys of Bordeaux wines.

One unforgettable day in 1972, a friend opened a 1962 Haut-Brion, the only *premier cru* bottle he had in his cellar; the label alone had sent him into reveries for years. Until this moment, my favorite tipples had consisted of Champagne and a few Sauternes, but with this wine's unusual and imitable aroma, persistent flavor, and velvety tannins, I became an instant convert to the world of fine reds.

I immediately sought out other wines from the region to taste, notably from the indescribably chaotic cellars of my Bacchic mentor, Jean-Baptiste Besse, on rue de la Montagne Sainte-Geneviève, the paradise lost of every former student from the neighboring universities.

It wasn't until a good decade later that I finally understood the secretive, discreetly subtle, and elegant nature of the most characteristic wines of the 1960s—such as the 1962 and 1964 Haut-Bailly and Domaine de Chevalier—which we owe to the brilliant wine-making and blending talents of Emile Peynaud, the forefather of modern oenology. Defending these wines against the skepticism of countless amateurs who, in their near-monastic sobriety, drank them too young and denied themselves communion with Bordeaux's most unique and irreplaceable heritage, simply enhanced my appreciation of them.

By comparing the sensations offered by the wide palette of colors, textures, and flavors found in Girondin vintages, it is simple to see just how exceptional the wines from Graves really are. The mature, round character of the great Merlots from Libournais often call to mind fine Burgundy or Rhône wines, especially in warm years. The spicy cedar flavors of Médocs can also regularly be found, sometimes to an extreme, in most of the wonderful Cabernet Sauvignons from the New World.

Wines from Graves, however, constitute the heart and soul of Bordeaux wines, the sum of their most inimitable parts. Yet learning to identify and appreciate them requires a thorough grounding, which can demand some effort if your formative years were shaped by wines from other regions. First, they have a discreet yet distinct and assertive fruitiness, particularly in *nouveau* wines. This quality easily surpasses any varietal character, bringing out the complex and complementary varieties that go into the majority of these wines; Merlot, for instance, blends so well with Cabernets from Graves, whose tannins are so much rounder and softer than their counterparts in Médoc.

There is the influence of the Landaise Forest and its pine- and acacia-scented air, whose flavor predominates in the grapes that pickers munch while harvesting. In windy years, the air penetrates the red fruit aromas of the red grapes and the white and yellow fruit aromas of the white grapes. The Cabernet Sauvignons and their white cousin Sauvignon are the grapes most affected by this phenomenon and their finely musky note is found nowhere else. In Pessac, this slight muskiness is accompanied by the whimsical, infuriating hints of soot, creosote, and smoke that appear one day and mysteriously disappear the next, in some years even transported by unknown means to the furthest boundaries of Léognan.

The very composition of these long-aging wines is in perfect keeping with the geographic location of the wine-growing region, on the edge of the 45th parallel, between ocean, forest, and river. "Balance" is the word that best describes these wines: never over the top, nothing declamatory or insistent in their aromas or tactile sensations, an impression of radiant intimacy more than brazen, bold-faced manufacture; order, beauty, and calm, but never sensuousness. Even Baudelaire, deeply traditional because

of his education and sensibility, would not have denigrated them in their glorious stage of maturity, when their light and scent of beautiful autumnal Aquitaine sunsets fill the glass and exquisitely confuse our senses.

The region's white wines, both admired and criticized for their infamous unpredictability once bottled, are an equally complex subject. In their first flushes of youth, thanks to contemporary wine-making methods, honed to capture the slightest aromatic nuance from the grape, the white wines have an appealing charm and vivacity and never compromise on strength or density. Redolent of fresh air and sunlight on the ocean, they are wines to enjoy in spring and summer; but, like an albatross, they are ungainly on terra firma or in confined spaces. Then there is a long, bleak period when the wine rebels, sulks, and sometimes smells bad, a quality oenologists explain away with terms like "reduction." The furious amateur will swear never to drink these wines again and quickly take refuge in the comfortable and uninspiring company of every Chardonnay on the planet. Finally, one fine day (although we never know too far ahead which one), the wine suddenly awakens, as no other wine in the world can, and brings its constituent parts together in a coating of acacia or pine honey with a splash of ocean spray, inviting us to pair it with a line-caught wild bass, crayfish, or lobster worthy of it.

The greatest wines from Graves are the *Crus Classés*, reclassified in 1959 after changes to the initial 1953 classification. They cover just over 600 hectares, which is not much when we consider the scale of the other great terroirs in France, even in Bordeaux alone, and the massive, ever-growing global market. At the request of the Graves producers, the legislature changed their civil status, bestowing on them the Pessac-Léognan appellation, the only one to combine the names of two independent communes. But an appellation, particularly in Bordeaux, owes much of its status to the vineyards within its limits: in the case of Graves, the various vineyards have never been so well defended, primarily by the activism and personal charisma of the individual property owners.

In contrast with other regions, each château is an estate wine and a home to the winegrower, who enjoys living near the city of Bordeaux and all its attractions. Living on site allows growers to keep constant watch over the vines, the development of the wine, and the work of their staff on the estate. It also allows them to welcome visitors, professionals, and wine lovers in person with warmth and hospitality. By showing a sense of family, similar to other French wine-growing regions, the growers of these grand vintage wines show a more relaxed, human side of Bordeaux, more likely to bring an end to the facile prejudices that have sprung from history, chance, and necessity over the years and that

would otherwise turn the big châteaux into cold, nameless monuments.

Remember too that being close to the Landes district also means the hosts are fond of food, more concerned than their Gironde counterparts with pleasing guests by selecting dishes that show the wines in their best light.

Yet the natural ease with which they carry out their determined efforts to defend and showcase their heritage also owes a great deal to their innate humanity, their generosity and love of sharing and talking, and to the fact that they are relatively few in number and thus cherish every opportunity to get together. Collectively, all of these winegrowers—some for generations, others more recently but nevertheless as deeply rooted to their lands—form a very united, even friendly front, which is quite astonishing in a world where special interests typically breed self-interest. The glue that binds them is clearly their desire to defend their classification—as their counterparts in Médoc or Sauternes did in 1855—a classification that is well worth defending and of which they are truly deserving by the value of their soil, hard work, and remarkable wines. This book will help you understand what makes them legendary.

Château Haut-Brion

A pioneering estate from the 1530s on, Château Haut-Brion is the ro
model for fine red Graves and Bordeaux. The first property
to be known by its place name, Haut-Brion fashioned
the "New French Claret" in the 17th century and over the years
has continued to be in the forefront in terms
of quality, style, and innovation.

A trailblazer from its inception in the early 16th century, Château Haut-Brion is an exemplary estate for fine red Graves and Bordeaux. The first property to be known by its place name, Haut-Brion created the "New French Claret" in the 17th century and over the years has continued to be a leader in quality, style, and innovation. Crucial to its consistency and success have been an exceptional terroir, dedicated ownership, and the intelligent use of technology.

Once a country retreat, the 51-hectare estate is now encircled by the commune of Pessac, southwest of the city of Bordeaux. The vineyard is formed on two southeast-facing sand and gravel knolls; like many of the major sites in Bordeaux, it has the essential elements of gently sloping hills, deep, poor, gravelly soil, and a

well drained subsoil composed of limestone and clay.

In certain areas the gravel has been eroded by the passage of two streams, the Serpent and the Peugue, allowing the limestone and clay to outcrop. In others sand has been moved by gravity and erosion and deposited at the bottom of the slopes. This adds to the complexity of the terrain. The "inner city" location provides slightly higher average annual temperatures than surrounding areas, meaning that Haut-Brion grapes ripen earlier.

Even the best terroir needs careful nurturing, and in this respect Haut-Brion has been well served. Successive proprietors and managers have provided continuity, direction, and a consistent desire for perfection.

Preceding pages:
The front view of Château Haut-Brion as it has appeared on the label of this cru for over a century.
Below:
The *cuvier* in 1924.
Opposite, top right:
Clarence Dillon, painted by Philip Alexius de Laszlo in 1926.
Opposite, bottom left:
H.R.H. Prince Robert of Luxembourg.

The estate's initial success and renown can be attributed to the de Pontac family, which directly and then through the female line owned Haut-Brion until the Revolution. Jean de Pontac, the founder, established the estate from a dowry of land brought by his wife, Jeanne de Bellon, and the *maison noble* of Haut-Brion, which he acquired in 1533. He later added other parcels of land and in 1549 began construction of the château, the manor of which remains today.

A century later his descendant Arnaud III de Pontac further enhanced the reputation of the property. A wealthy and politically powerful figure (he became First President of the Bordeaux Parliament in 1653), he oversaw improvements in wine-making standards and, with his son François-Auguste, consolidated the market for the wine in England. The 1660 cellar ledger of King Charles II bears witness to this, as do the words penned by the chronicler Samuel Pepys

in 1663: "I drank a sort of French wine, called Ho Bryan [sic], that hath a good and most particular taste that I ever met with."

François-Auguste de Pontac had no heirs, and on his death Haut-Brion was divided, two-thirds passing through the female line to the de Fumel family. Joseph de Fumel (1720–1794) continued to invest in the property, adding a park, an orangery, and other buildings. It was during this time that Haut-Brion was visited by Thomas Jefferson, who described it as one of the "four vineyards of prime quality" in Bordeaux.

Joseph de Fumel was guillotined during the Revolution and the property confiscated. It was later restored to the family, who sold it to the French Foreign Minister, Talleyrand, in 1801. His ownership was short-lived, and the property was resold several times before being acquired

by Joseph Eugène Larrieu in 1836. Under his stewardship the domaine returned to its original size prior to the division in 1694 and was classed *Premier Cru* in the 1855 classification.

The estate stayed in the Larrieu family until 1922. After a period of economic difficulty, stability and continuity were restored when the American Clarence Dillon purchased the property in 1935. His great-grandson, H.R.H. Prince Robert of Luxembourg, is President of the estate today. This period has also been marked by the dedication of the Estate Managers, the Delmas family: Georges (1923), his son Jean-Bernard (1961), and his son Jean-Philippe (2004).

Another element that has kept Haut-Brion ahead of the game is the owners' ready use of new technology and techniques for viticulture and wine-making. In the 17th century the proximity to the city of Bordeaux and the power and

wealth of the de Pontac family allowed for these advances. *Ouillage* and *soutirage* were current practices, as was the use of sulfur for sterilizing barrels. Perhaps a greater effort in the vineyard—smaller yields, the rejection of moldy grapes—also contributed to the wines' noted quality.

More recently Haut-Brion took the "revolutionary" step of introducing stainless steel fermentation tanks in 1961, then built another state-of-the-art *cuverie* in 1991, while in the vineyards a groundbreaking program of clonal selection has been in place since the 1970s. Fine tuning today continues in the hands of Jean-Philippe Delmas and the experienced team of *Maitre de Chai* Jean-Philippe Masclef and *Chef de Culture* Pascal Baratié.

The Haut-Brion vineyard now has an average age of just over 35 years and is planted to 44 percent Cabernet Sauvignon, 45 percent Merlot,

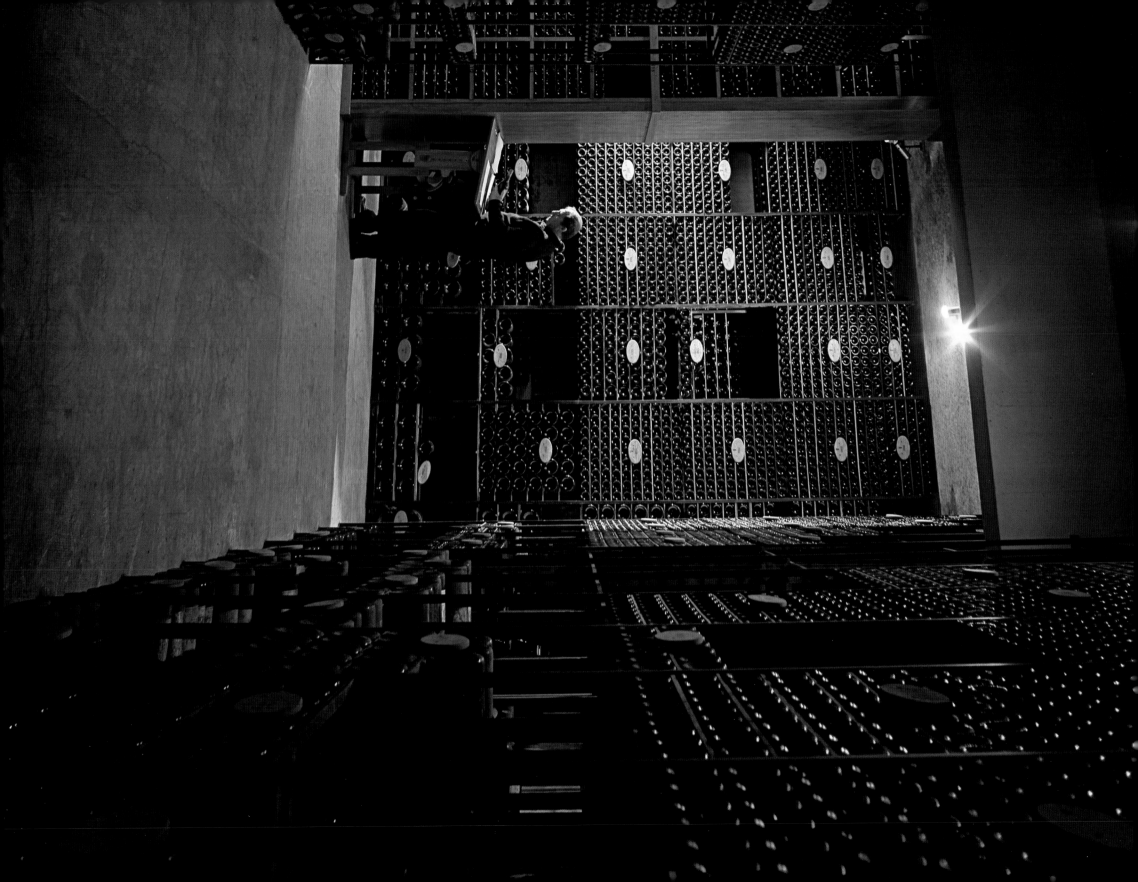

10 percent Cabernet Franc, and 1 percent Petit Verdot. In reality, though, Merlot generally amounts to 55 percent of the blend, contributing to Haut-Brion's characteristically smooth, round, unctuous texture. Only 50 percent of the production is selected for the *grand vin*, the rest destined for the second wine, Le Clarence de Haut-Brion (Château Bahans Haut-Brion until the 2006 vintage), or the generic label.

Elegance, more than anything, is the hallmark of Haut-Brion, something that is clearly evident even in the lesser years. The quality and finesse of tannin is exceptional and the bouquet complex but harmonious, with roasted, burnt, cocoa bean, and caramel notes and an almost overripe fruit character. This makes the wine seductive when young, which occasionally belies its considerable potential to age.

A tiny amount of white Haut-Brion is also produced from a little less than three hectares of vineyard. Somewhat surprisingly, the wine is not classified. It is rich, full, and intense but with balancing acidity, the dominance of Sauvignon Blanc (55 percent) providing a pungent citrus aroma in the wine's youth.

Preceding pages: Jean-Philippe Masclef, Oenologist and *Maître de chai* in the old vintages cellar.

Daniel Boulud

Roasted Squab with Foie Gras, Peppered Apricots, Spinach, and Turnip Confit

Ingredients
Serves 4

For the Apricots
- 8 ripe apricots, cut in half and pitted, 4 pits crushed and reserved
- 3 tablespoons (65 g) honey
- 1 tablespoon (15 ml) freshly squeezed lemon juice
- Pinch (¼ teaspoon) cracked black pepper

For the Vegetables
- 3 tablespoons (45 g) unsalted butter
- 12 baby turnips, peeled, greens trimmed to 5 ½ inch (1.5 cm)
- 1 cup (240 ml) unsalted chicken stock
- Salt and freshly ground pepper
- ½ pound (225 g) spinach, stems and tough center veins removed, well washed, and dried
- 1 clove garlic, peeled and crushed

For the Squab
- 4 ¾-pound (350 g) squabs
- 4 ounces (115 ml) crème fraîche
- Pinch (¼ teaspoon) coriander seeds
- Pinch (¼ teaspoon) freshly grated nutmeg
- Pinch (¼ teaspoon) Thai peppercorns, crushed
- 1 tablespoon (15 ml) extra-virgin olive oil
- 1 tablespoon (15 g) unsalted butter
- 1 shallot, peeled, trimmed, finely chopped, and rinsed
- 2 pinches (½ teaspoon) cracked black pepper
- 2 tablespoons (30 ml) brandy
- 1 tablespoon (15 ml) amaretto
- 2 cups (480 ml) unsalted chicken stock
- ½ pound (220 g) fresh foie gras, cleaned and cut into 4 pieces

For the Apricots. Center a rack in the oven and preheat the oven to 350°F (175°C). Butter a 9 x 9-inch (23 x 23-cm) square baking pan. Place the apricots, cut side up, in the pan. Drizzle with the honey and lemon juice, and sprinkle with the pepper. Slide the pan into the oven and bake until the apricots are tender, 10 to 15 minutes depending on the ripeness of the apricots. Remove and set aside.

For the Vegetables. Melt 2 tablespoons (30 g) of the butter in a large sauté pan over medium-high heat. Add the turnips and cook for 2 to 3 minutes. Add the chicken stock, cover the pan, and cook until the turnips are tender, approximately 10 minutes. Season with salt and pepper. Transfer the turnips to a plate and keep warm. Wipe the pan clean with a paper towel. Melt the remaining 1 tablespoon (15 g) of butter in the same pan over high heat. Add the spinach and garlic, and season to taste with salt and pepper. Toss until the spinach is tender but still bright green, about 5 minutes. Discard the garlic and drain off any liquid remaining in the pan. Set aside and keep warm.

For the Squab. Remove the wing joints, legs, and breasts from the squab. Debone the thighs and the legs. Reserve all the livers and the carcasses. In a spice grinder, crush together the coriander seeds, nutmeg, and Thai peppercorns. Combine the spices and crème fraîche together. Spread the mixture over the breasts and marinate overnight in the refrigerator.

Place a rack in the top position of the oven and preheat the broiler. Wrap the thighs in aluminum foil. Place the marinated squab breasts and thighs on the rack of the broiler pan and broil the breasts on each side until the skin is golden brown, approximately 5 minutes. Remove from the oven. Let the squabs rest for 5 minutes.

Cut the reserved carcasses into small pieces. Warm the olive oil in a medium sauté pan over medium-high heat. Add the carcasses and the reserved livers. Reduce the heat to medium and add the butter, shallots, and cracked pepper. Cook until the shallots are tender but have no color, 10 to 12 minutes. Add the apricot halves and the crushed pits, and continue to cook, while stirring, until the apricots become a little mushy. Deglaze with the brandy and amaretto and cook until the liquid is reduced by half. Add the chicken stock and simmer for 30 minutes. Strain the sauce through a fine-mesh sieve, taste, and season with salt, if necessary. Set aside and keep warm.

Season the foie gras with salt and pepper. Set a heavy sauté pan over high heat and sear the foie gras for 2 to 3 minutes on each side.

If necessary, reheat the spinach and turnips. In a 375°F (190°C) oven reheat the squab breasts for 2 minutes on each side. Cut each breast in half. Place a mound of spinach on the center of each of four warm dinner plates. Arrange the squab breast and two legs on top along with a piece of foie gras. Season the meat with rock salt. Drizzle the sauce around the plate and scatter the apricots and turnips around. Serve immediately.

Château Haut-Brion rouge 2005

This noble, full-bodied wine is matched in refinement by the squab en salmis. Not only do the rich flavors of the squab soften this wine's powerful structure, but the gaminess of the bird sings with the smoky, earthy aromas of the Haut-Brion.

—Daniel Johnnes, Sommelier

Château Bouscaut

Surrounded by vines, Château Bouscaut stands proudly among the 300-year-old oak trees on the magnificent grounds, bearing witness to the longstanding history of this domain. This beautiful, stately 19th-century home was partly destroyed then rebuilt after a fire in the 1960s. With its cellars, Bouscaut enjoys a panoramic view across the 47-hectare vineyard that runs adjacent to the road linking Bordeaux to Toulouse.

Château Bouscaut's vineyard dates back to the 16th century, when it was known as Haut-Truchon. Its past becomes clearer toward the end of the 19th century with the Chabanneau family, who renamed it Bouscaut, as it was known locally. Production increased from 40 barrels (48,000 bottles) of red wine in 1881 to 100 (120,000 bottles) by 1908.

By the time it was acquired by the Comte de Rivaud and Victor Place in 1925, Bouscaut was considered a model estate, as testified by a statement from the chairman of a jury presenting the Prime d'honneur award on behalf of the Ministry of Agriculture in 1926: "This property, almost exclusively viticultural, is superbly maintained. Overall—vines, wines and cellars—it has achieved perfection; admirably well situated,

homogenous, equipped with modern, luxurious barrel cellars and vat-room, it impresses the visitor who is eager to see progress."

Under the guidance of Victor Place, as much a socialite as a renowned winemaker, the production of white wines intensified. The château's regulars—French music stars like Louis Jouvet, Gilbert Bécaud, and Charles Trénet—were already singing its praises.

Place remained at the helm of the property until its sale to a group of American investors in 1968. Anne-Marie Delmas, the wife of the director of Château Haut-Brion, Jean-Bernard Delmas, was then appointed to manage Bouscaut. In 1979 Lucien Lurton, one of the greatest Bordeaux winemakers, who is deeply

Opposite:
Dawn harvests.

40

Opposite:
A vineyard manager
watches over grape-
pickers.

attached to the finest terroirs, became the owner. He undertook a vast project to renew the vineyards, finishing in 1990 with the construction of a circular vinification cellar and a barrel cellar.

In 1992 Lucien Lurton surprised all and sundry by handing over his many estates to his ten children. Sophie Lurton and her brother Louis received Château Bouscaut. She has since taken over complete ownership and manages the property with her husband, Laurent Cogombles, an agricultural engineer who is as passionate about wine as she is.

Sophie's débuts at the head of Bouscaut were far from easy: three difficult vintages (1992, 1993, 1994), buying her brother Louis' shares, and the large investments needed to modernize

it were a heavy weight to bear, but Sophie and Laurent's tenacity has borne fruit.

Merlot is perfectly suited to the limestone-clay soils and makes up 50 percent of the red plantings. Due to the strategy of low yields and careful grape selection, the Château Bouscaut Merlots possess a color, a quality of tannin, and a power that are worthy of this terroir.

The Cabernet Sauvignon represents 45 percent of the red grapes and is planted on gravelly outcrops using meticulously chosen rootstocks, bringing structured elegance to the wine. The remaining 5 percent is Malbec (rather surprising in Bordeaux). Planted in the 1960s, it brings energy, full body, and gorgeous spicy notes to the wine.

Preceding pages:
The fruit of painstaking work
at all levels.
Below:
Sophie Lurton-Cogombles
and Laurent Cogombles.

As with the red wine, the white became a classified growth in 1953 and has greatly contributed to the château's reputation. Sauvignon Blanc and Sémillon are planted on 7 hectares of clayey-calcareous soil, which is particularly suited to these varietals. Despite the recent flurry for Sauvignon Blanc in Bordeaux, Sémillon still has a special place at Bouscaut with 50 percent of the white plantings, including one block planted before 1900.

The Sémillon endows Bouscaut's white wines with fullness and finesse that are amplified by using oak barrels for both the fermentation and aging. Complemented by the freshness and fruitiness of the Sauvignon Blanc, the wine is both gorgeous while young and able to age beautifully.

At Château Bouscaut the wines are a perfect blend of tradition and modernity, a reflection of the strong character of the terroir and the deep convictions of its owners.

Christopher Coutanceau
Bass in Shellfish Foam with Duck and Lemon Jus

For the Shellfish. Pan-fry the abalones, clams, and razor clams in the escargot butter. Keep the shellfish warm.

For the Gnocchi. Boil the potatoes. Peel them while still hot and push them through a potato ricer. Stir in the basil, grated nutmeg, flour, and egg. Season and mix well. Chill the mixture in the refrigerator for 1 hour.

Once the mixture has chilled, form small balls and press them down with the back of a fork. Simmer in salted water: allow 1 tablespoon (10 g) of coarse sea salt for each quart of water. The gnocchi are done when they rise to the surface. Drain and leave the gnocchi to cool in iced water. Refrigerate.

For the Shellfish Foam. Reduce the shellfish jus (or fish stock) by half and blend in the milk and cream. Reduce the mixture by half again and then add the butter. Season to taste. Keep warm.

Reduce the duck jus (or chicken stock) until you have 1 ⅔ cups (400 ml). Add the butter, olive oil, and preserved lemon. Leave to infuse and season to taste. Keep warm.

Just before serving, pan-fry the bass fillets 8 minutes on the skin side and then 2 minutes on the opposite side. Plate the fish and arrange the shellfish neatly around the bass. Add the lettuce, lightly dressed in olive oil. Emulsify the shellfish foam and pour over the shellfish. Pour a drizzle of duck jus around the bass. Serve immediately.

Ingredients
Serves 8

For the Shellfish
- 24 abalone slices
- 32 clams
- 32 razor clams
- 3 tablespoons (50 g) escargot butter
- 2 ¾ pounds (1.2 kg) line-caught wild bass divided into 5-ounce (150 g) fillets
- 16 sucrine lettuce heads
- Olive oil
- Salt and freshly ground pepper

For the Basil Gnocchi
- 9 ounces (250 g) Mona Lisa potatoes
- 1 ounce (30 g) finely chopped basil
- Freshly grated nutmeg
- 1 cup (150 g) all-purpose flour
- 1 egg
- Fleur de sel (coarse sea salt)

For the Shellfish Foam
- 2 cups (500 ml) shellfish jus (or fish stock made from a dry base)
- 1 cup (250 ml) whole milk
- 1 cup (250 ml) single cream
- ¼ cup plus 2 tablespoons (100 g) unsalted butter

For the Duck and Lemon Jus
- 1 quart (1 liter) reduced duck jus (or chicken stock)
- ¼ cup plus 2 tablespoons (100 g) unsalted butter
- 3 tablespoons olive oil
- 2 preserved lemons, cut into chunks

Château Bouscaut blanc 2005

This wine is chick-yellow with silver highlights and a rather exuberant nose of white peach and vine peach. When oxidized, the aromas of orange blossom, citrus, bitter almonds, and a hint of vanilla come through. Initially on the palate it is quite bitter and almondy, and the harshness of unripe peach gives an acid finish. It has some fatness and perfect length. This wine should be decanted if you want to drink it now, or left for three or four years.
In this wild bass dish, the fish rounds out the wine's bitter, fresh character, while the slightly nutty and lemony duck jus brings out the almond aromas, each revealing and harmonizing with the other without dominating. A truly great wine matched by a fine and flavorful dish!
Serve at 48–52°F (9–11°C).

—Nicolas Brossard, Sommelier

Château Carbonnieux

Impressive both in size and history, this property has 90 hectares under vine, split between red and white, and a lineage that can be traced back to the 13th century. The Perrin family, which ushered in the modern era when it took over in 1956, continues to bring renown to this prestigious name.

Château Carbonnieux may be one of the oldest estates in Pessac-Léognan, but it has the air of a going concern today. It boasts 90 hectares under production, almost equally split between red and white wines, a state-of-the-art winery, a good distribution system, and an attractive 13th-century château (actually a fortified country manor) that has become a welcoming family home.

This was not the case in 1956, when Marc Perrin purchased the property. The vineyard was in shambles, with only 30 hectares under vine, and a terrible frost that year was followed by three unproductive years. The château had been uninhabited since the 1920s and the cellars and equipment were in need of repair. Sales and distribution were uncertain.

It required courage to think long-term, but having been *vignerons* since at least 1830, the Perrin family perhaps had some perspective on the task before them. Marc and his son Antony worked tirelessly to restore Carbonnieux to its former glory, bringing a modern approach and a commitment to quality wine-making and viticulture as well as to the name Carbonnieux.

When Antony Perrin died in 2008, his sons Eric and Philibert took over the family business. The Perrins have left their stamp on Carbonnieux, but many others have contributed to the development and reputation of the property during its long history, including the de Ferron family, Benedictine monks, Jean-Baptiste and Henri-Xavier Bouchereau, and Dr. Georges Martin.

Opposite, bottom right:
Philibert and Eric Perrin.

The viticultural history of Carbonnieux can be traced back as far as the 13th century. It has been established that during this era Benedictine monks procured an income from vines cultivated at the "Plantier de Carbonnieux" in the parish of Léognan. The name probably derived from the Carbonius family, who helped clear the forest and plant the land.

The real birth of the domaine, though, occurred in the 16th century with the arrival of the de Ferron family: Jean de Ferron and later his son, Jean-Charles, gradually increased the family holdings in the area, and Jean-Charles took the title of *seigneur* of Carbonnieux around 1540.

Documentation from the 17th century provides evidence that wine from Carbonnieux was sold via courtiers in Bordeaux and to *négociants* in Brittany. During this period Carbonnieux had become a considerable estate (approximately

115 hectares), but mismanagement eventually led to its decline; the last of the de Ferrons sold the property to the Benedictine order of the Abbaye Sainte-Croix de Bordeaux in 1740.

The return of the Benedictines led to a focus on wine production to the exclusion of other farming activities. The vineyard was increased to 50 hectares (in a single parcel around the château), making it the largest viticultural estate in the Graves. Under the Benedictines' ownership Carbonnieux established a reputation for its white wines, which were considered equal to the reds of Château Haut-Brion at the time. Bottled at the estate, these wines were praised for their clarity and limpidity.

When the French Revolution brought an end to ecclesiastical ownership, the estate was duly confiscated and sold at auction to the Bouchereau family. The brothers Jean-Baptiste

Château Carbonnieux

55

and Henri-Xavier Bouchereau maintained the estate's high quality, particularly with the whites, and enlarged the estate to 178 hectares. Château Carbonnieux, as it was now known, became a "model domaine" and was visited by many.

From 1871 to 1894 Carbonnieux had several owners. The most notable of these was Dr. Georges Martin, who helped Carbonnieux to recover after the phylloxera infestation in the late 19th century (and would later found the first Graves de Bordeaux winegrowers association in 1904). The estate changed hands again in 1920 and after the Second World War. Although the estate's red and white wines were classified in 1953, by 1956 Carbonnieux was in need of a restorative hand.

When the Perrins took over, they immediately launched a program of replanting, which intensified after 1962. The vineyard is situated on a gravel outcrop with pockets of sand, gravel, and limestone as the slope falls away. Over the years the Perrins have planted Sauvignon Blanc (65 percent) and Sémillion (35 percent) on the clay-limestone soil, while the deeper gravel of the higher land has been reserved for Cabernet Sauvignon.

Until 1987 the white wines were vinified in stainless steel tanks; barrel fermentation, under the direction of consultant oenologist and white wine specialist Professor Denis Dubourdieu, was introduced in 1988. A quarter of the barrels are renewed each year. The minerality that was detected back in the 18th century is still there,

along with notes of citrus and pear. The wine displays a modern concentration of fruit and a clean, dry, well-balanced finish.

As the vineyard has matured, so has the quality of the red wine, particularly after the inauguration of a new *cuverie* in 1990. Cabernet Sauvignon (60 percent), Merlot (30 percent), Cabernet Franc (7 percent), Petit Verdot and Malbec (3 percent) are included in the blend. Carbonnieux red is a typical Graves with a fresh, well-structured palate, notes of dark fruit and well-integrated oak. It still has a surprising ability to age.

Éric Briffard

Golden Diver Scallops in Colombo Spice Cauliflower Bulgur with Carica

Ingredients
Serves 2

- 3½ ounces (100g) cauliflower florets (1 to 1½ cups)
- 1 teaspoon white balsamic vinegar
- 3 to 4 pinches Colombo powder
- Salt and white pepper
- Olive oil
- 3½ ounces (100g) carica or mango
- 2 soft, dried apricots
- 1 tomato, peeled, seeded, and cut into small cubes
- 3 fresh cilantro leaves
- 1 ounce (30g) blanched Corinth grapes
- 3½ ounces (100g) gray prawns
- 2¾ pounds (1.2kg) diver scallops in their shells
- 2 to 3 pinches curry powder
- 1 lemongrass stalk
- Zest and juice of 1 lime
- 1½ tablespoons (25g) unsalted butter
- Fresh chives

Chop the cauliflower florets with a knife until they resemble a fairly coarse bulgur. Season with the vinegar, Colombo powder, salt, white pepper, and olive oil. Set aside.

Peel the carica (or mango) and cut 4 round slices of the fruit. Set aside. Chop the remaining fruit into small cubes. Chop the dried apricots and tomatoes into cubes. In a bowl, mix them with 2 finely chopped cilantro leaves, then combine with the cubed carica (or mango) and half of the Corinth grapes. Pour the resulting mixture into small steel rings about 1½ inches (4 cm) in diameter. Press the mixture down, and top each ring with a round slice of carica (or mango). Gloss the top with a coating of olive oil.

Shell the gray prawns, cutting off and reserving the heads. Put the prawn heads in a small saucepan and pour in enough water to cover them. Simmer for 10 minutes and then strain. Set aside.

Open the scallop shells with a knife and remove the scallops. Clean them and remove the beards. Wash the beards.

In a sauté pan, fry the beards with a drizzle of olive oil, 1 or 2 pinches of curry powder, the lemongrass stalk, lime zest, prawn jus, and ½ cup (100ml) of water. Let reduce by half, and then add a knob of butter. Reduce again until you obtain a syrupy consistency. Strain the sauce. Add the prawns, the scallop beards, the remaining Corinth grapes, a few drops of lime juice, and 1 chopped cilantro leaf. Set aside.

Season the scallops with a pinch of curry powder. Heat up a drizzle of olive oil in a sauté pan. Cook the scallops for 30 seconds, turn them over and add a knob of butter. Remove from the heat when the scallops are half-cooked.

Arrange 3 scallops and 2 bulgur stacks on long plates. Dress with the sauce and garnish with the bards and prawns. Decorate with a few fresh chive stalks, coarsely chopped. Serve immediately.

Château Carbonnieux blanc 2005

Selected from a complex and intense vintage year, this fine wine—produced from Sauvignon Blanc (more than 60 percent) and Sémillon grapes—strikes a perfect chord with the scallops in this dish. The aromas of white fruit and almonds add a further layer to the dish's range of spicy notes. Maturing the wine in barrels and stirring the lees (or *bâtonnage*) give the wine body and balance. Freshness and acidity come from a combination of the Sauvignon and the terroir. This assemblage blends marvelously with the natural sweetness of the pearly scallops. The firm cauliflower bulgur is the ideal contrast to the generous character of this 2005 vintage.
To best appreciate this pairing and let the wine express itself fully, serve at 50–54°F (10–12°C).

—Thierry Hamon, Sommelier

Domaine de Chevalier

The best way to describe Domaine de Chevalier is a vast glade covered with vines. The pine forest encroaches on three sides, the softly undulating vineyard taking center stage, with only the stone of the château and cellar complex interrupting the abundant greenery. Isolated from neighboring estates and a less than ideal property for cultivating the vine, Chevalier is a wonderful example of how man can affect a terroir.

The first to shape the form and reputation of Domaine de Chevalier was Jean Ricard. In 1865 he and his father, Arnaud, both coopers, purchased the 44-hectare property, which was then known by the Gascon name "Chivaley." Viticulture was a minor activity, but noting that vines had been planted here since the 17th century and appeared again at a later date on Belleyme's 18th-century map, Ricard expanded the vineyard to 15 hectares and changed the name to the French "Chevalier."

Well established by the late 19th century, Chevalier's stature was further enhanced from 1900 on under the management of Ricard's son-in-law, Gabriel Beaumartin. A successful businessman in his own right, he increased the vineyard to 18 hectares, built cellars, and advanced the wine's reputation as one of the top Graves.

In 1948 Jean Ricard's son, Claude, a young musician fresh from studies at the Paris Conservatoire, took over the reins. A dirt road to the winery and well water for drinking provided a stark contrast to the urbanity of Paris, but the 21-year-old was drawn to the property and over the next 35 years made his mark on the estate. Assisted by eminent oenologist Emile Peynaud, he further improved the quality of the wines, particularly the white, introducing a strict procedure for harvesting and adding a drainage system to the vineyard in 1962.

The human story of Domaine de Chevalier continues with the purchase of the property by

One unique feature of Domaine de Chevalier is that, in a relatively short space of time, it has achieved a level of renown that the great growths of Bordeaux have taken centuries to attain.

It is our assurance that nowhere else are grapes sorted with such painstaking attention.

the Bernard family in 1983 and the arrival of 23-year-old Olivier Bernard at the helm. A resident manager, he, like Claude Ricard, has lived the adventure to the fullest over the years, trying to understand, express, and improve the essence of Chevalier.

The proximity of the forest to the vineyard and consequent extremes of temperature result in zones that are prone to spring frost (prior to the sale Chevalier was hit in 1980, 1981, and 1982), particularly those planted with earlier-ripening white varieties. To ameliorate the situation, trees immediately surrounding the vineyard have been cut down, five

wind machines installed, and smudge pots introduced.

The soil is mainly gravelly black sand over a subsoil of clay and gravel mixed with iron-rich sandstone—an adequate base for viticulture provided there's a guiding hand. In the last 25 years, a steady program of restructuring and replanting has been followed, with the density of planting increased to 10,000 vines per hectare, the Sauvignon Blanc consigned to cooler zones, and the Cabernet Sauvignon located on the deeper, warmer, more gravelly soils. Plowing and sustainable agriculture have become de rigueur and the yields restrained.

The size of the vineyard has now more than doubled, to 47 hectares under vine. Six of these are planted with Sauvignon Blanc (70 percent) and Sémillon (30 percent) for Chevalier's amazing white wines. Long, pure, and crystalline, these seem to defy time, achieving remarkable consistency in both the good and more "delicate" years. Offering citrus and floral notes in youth, they evolve toward wax, quince, peach, and honeyed aromas with age, always with an underlying mineral quality that provides freshness and adds complexity.

The wine-making is meticulous, to say the least. After a selection process in the vineyard that is as strict as at top Sauternes estates, the grapes are pressed and the juice is cold settled, then fermented in oak barrels, 35 percent of which are renewed each year. The wine spends 18 months in barrel, longer than any other dry white in Bordeaux, where it takes on weight and texture and undergoes a natural clarification.

The red is produced in a circular cellar that was built in 1991. Cabernet Sauvignon (64

A vertical tasting of the last 30 vintages from the estate will show there has not been any digression. Man is but an enlightener —the terroir dominates everything.

"I let the wine lead me, while continually looking for balance; I never deny the importance of the modern world, but neither do I ignore the idea of a certain past, a certain history…."

Olivier Bernard

percent) is the principal variety, supplemented by Merlot (30 percent), Cabernet Franc, and Petit Verdot (3 percent each). This is a wine of great finesse, somewhat Médocain in style, again with minerality and smoky black currant notes. Vintages since 1996 have exhibited greater purity of fruit and acquired additional volume on the palate.

In a relatively short time, as far as the history of Bordeaux is concerned, Domaine de Chevalier has risen to the upper echelon of *crus*. Although man was necessary to mold the ingredients, the style of the wine is as defined as the terroir.

Michel Trama
The Famous Potato en Papillote with Truffle Sauce

Ingredients
Serves 4

- 4 potatoes
- 8 large chard leaves
- 2 ¾ ounces (80 g) truffle (2 to 3 truffles)
- 1 cup (250 g) chicken or vegetable stock
- ½ cup (4 ¼ ounces) (120 g) truffle juice
- 8 tablespoons (1stick) (130 g) unsalted butter
- Salt and freshly ground pepper

For the Potatoes. Boil the potatoes in salted water, using 1 heaping tablespoon of salt per quart of water, for 30 to 40 minutes. The potatoes should be soft but firm. Leave them to cool before peeling.

Wash the chard leaves, removing the stalks, and blanch in boiling water. Immediately, cool the leaves in iced water and transfer to a clean tea towel to dry.

Using a mandoline, slice 28 truffle shavings for the potatoes and 4 extra for the garnish. Slice each potato crosswise into eight rounds. Season well with salt and pepper. Reassemble the potato, adding a truffle shaving between each round. Roll out a sheet of plastic wrap 12 x 12 inches (30 x 30 cm) on your work surface. Line the plastic wrap with chard leaves. Wrap each potato in the chard leaves. Tighten the plastic wrap around each potato.

For the Truffle Sauce. In a saucepan, reduce the chicken stock and truffle juice by one-third until you have approximately ⅔ cup (150 ml) of liquid. In another saucepan, place 1 ¾ ounces (50 g) of truffle to infuse in 2 tablespoons (30 g) of butter for 5 minutes. Combine with the remaining stock and truffle juice. Emulsify in a blender with 6 to 7 tablespoons (100 g) of butter to thicken the sauce. Season to taste. Steam the papillotes for 12 minutes, and then remove the plastic wrap.

Place each papillote in a warmed soup dish. Slice the potatoes lengthwise and dress with the truffle sauce. Place a truffle shaving on the center of each papillote as a finishing touch.

Domaine de Chevalier rouge 2005

This sophisticated dish of earthy, intense flavors needs a deep red wine that is minerally, powerful, and concentrated, with fine, complex aromas and dense, noble tannins. The Domaine de Chevalier 2005 has all of these qualities. In addition to an intense fruitiness, this wine offers a generous bouquet of notes, some balsamic, others slightly animal, but the aroma is above all fresh, conjuring up the scent of wet, smoky gravel. On the palate, the concentrated tannic structure, with a wonderful mineral freshness, strikes a perfect balance with the dish's complex, earthy, and animal flavors. The fondant potato and chicken stock, both strongly infused with truffle, marry superbly with the tight tannic structure and strength of the 2005 vintage. The wine isn't dominated, nor does it dominate; the balance is subtle. Together, the power of the wine and the richness of the dish create a final bouquet that is refreshed by the wine's acidity and heightened by the truffle's transcendent aroma.

Château Couhins

Stepping out of a period of relative obscurity, Couhins is making a return to the public domain. Research and studies of the vine have guided the estate's development in recent years; its wines are currently the preserve of the current owners, the Institut National de la Recherche Agronomique. Since 2006 wine lovers have been able to appreciate them again.

The reputation of Château Couhins ebbed and flowed in the late 20th century. Couhins was the same property as neighboring Couhins-Lurton until the estate was divided in 1968. Since then it has been owned by the Institut National de la Recherche Agronomique (INRA) and the vineyard has been greatly altered. The most recent development has been commercial, with the wines re-entering the public domain after a period of obscurity.

At the end of the 17th century the property was known as the "Bourdieu de la Gravette" and until 1805 was owned by the Banchereau family, wealthy *notaires* in the city of Bordeaux. Their principal production was red wines. Whites did not appear until the late 19th century, but they soon gained renown and were classified in 1959. At mid-century Couhins was a substantial estate of 60 hectares, some of which was acquired when the owner, Edouard

Gasqueton, amalgamated a second property, Château du Pont du Langon.

After the death of Gasqueton and a sequence of poor vintages in the 1960s, the property was put up for sale. INRA acquired 45 hectares of mostly abandoned vineyard. A mere two hectares were still under production, with the grapes being vinified by André Lurton until 1979. The château and cellars were purchased by a third party.

INRA is a government-funded body whose mission is to carry out "research for better food and nutrition, preservation of the environment and competitive, sustainable agricultural practices." Couhins was acquired as an experimental station, particularly with regard to sustainable viticulture, and its development has since been guided by research and studies of the vine.

Preceding pages:
A clay-limestone slope covered in Sauvignon Blanc vine stocks.
Above:
The barrel cellars and offices at Château Couhins before the planned refurbishment.
Opposite:
Sauvignon Blanc grapes are selectively harvested.

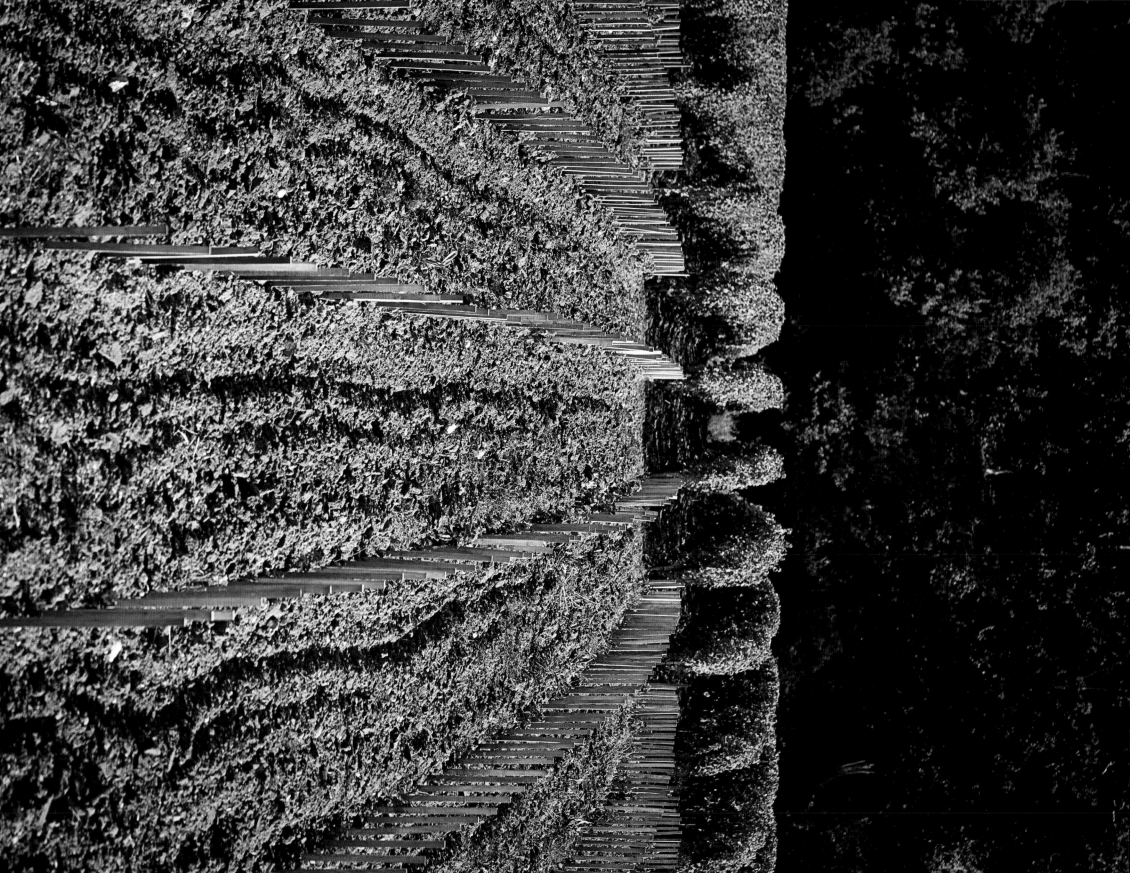

Château Couhins

Page 78, top left:
"Tasting the berries and observing the pips encourages the grapes to talk..." (Dominique Forget, Estate Director).

Top right:
Limestone rock peaks out from under a thin layer of clay; it helps the Sauvignon Blanc grapes to mature slowly but surely, guaranteeing their complex aromas.

Bottom right:
Harvest under the October sun (Brigitte Bourreau, Grape-Picking Team Manager).

Above:
In one area of the vineyard, INRA is implementing a new process for reducing vine treatments.

The first task was to restructure the vineyard's drains, ditches, and paths; the pattern of planting was eventually dictated by soil analysis. Three soil types were identified: a gravel hillock, which was planted with Cabernet Sauvignon; a zone of sand, gravel, and clay (resulting from erosion), planted with Merlot, Cabernet Sauvignon, and Petit Verdot; and a north-facing clay-limestone slope best suited to Sauvignon Blanc and Sémillon.

The principal themes of research at Couhins are precision viticulture and what is known as *production intégrée*, which aims to nurture soil through traditional methods like plowing and using compost. It also attempts to limit chemical treatments by taking into account the evolution of potential disease, the climate, and the vine's stage of development. The now-accepted method of confusing the grape moth by placing tiny vials of female pheromone in the vineyard, thus disrupting the moth's reproductive cycle, was first refined here.

Precision viticulture uses soil analysis—the ability to measure vine vigor and water content in the soil—to determine methods of cultivation in individual parcels of vines. Then the height of trellising can be changed, the system of pruning modified, and the use of fertilizers controlled. There are now well-documented histories of some of the parcels' berries (anthocyanins, sugar content, acidity, weight) available for study.

Through the initiation of these (originally) experimental projects, the vineyard has expanded over the years and now totals 23 hectares. Six are planted to white varieties (90 percent Sauvignon Blanc, 10 percent Sémillon) and 17 to red (50 percent Merlot, 40 percent Cabernet Sauvignon, 8 percent Cabernet Franc, 2 percent Petit Verdot).

A cellar for vinification and aging was constructed in 1981, and the wines have been made there since. The harvest date is determined by tasting the grapes and by gleaning information from precision viticulture.

The emphasis is very much on the expression of fruit, in particular the Sauvignon Blanc, grown on clay-limestone soils with a well-regulated supply of water and nitrogen. Grapefruit and passion fruit aromas come to the fore while the palate has a gentle fullness and flavor with a tingling line of acidity giving freshness on the finish.

Until recently the wines were sold privately, only to INRA personnel, but there is now a strong desire to rebuild the public image of Couhins. The entire production of the 2007 white was sold through the Place de Bordeaux for distribution around the world. A further step will be taken with the opening of a reception center in 2010 that will offer professionals the opportunity to visit the cellars and vineyard.

Page 81, top left:
Precise and targeted analyses to set the harvest date.

Top right:
An infrared sensor is used to map the vine vigor via GPS, precise to 1 sq.m.

Bottom left:
Map of the vine vigor of a parcel of Sauvignon Blanc: in 2008, areas of low vine vigor (yellow and light green) were at peak ripeness 12 days before the dark green areas and were therefore harvested and vinified separately.

Bottom right:
Attention to detail and precision are constant.

Opposite:
White wines being matured on fine lees (Hugues Roussarie, Vine and Barrel Cellar Technician).

Above left:
Benoît Fauconneau, President of INRA's center in Bordeaux Aquitaine.

Château Couhins

Pierre Gagnaire
Gilthead Bream and Liebig

Ingredients
Serves 6

- 3 cups (700 ml) white Couhins wine
- 1 cup (250 ml) olive oil
- 1 unsprayed organic grapefruit
- 4 gelatin leaves
- 2 cups (500 ml) spring water
- 1 ⅛ pounds (500 g) gilthead bream, sliced into thin strips
- Fleur de sel, preferably coarse sea salt from Guérande
- Salt and freshly ground pepper

For the Flavored Oil. Mix 2 cups (500 ml) of Couhins wine together with the olive oil in a bottle. Tightly seal it. Put the bottle in a bain-marie so that it is completely submerged in water for at least 1 hour, shaking the bottle regularly to ensure the flavor infuses through the oil. Then leave the bottle and its contents to cool completely before using. Divide the infused olive oil into two parts: ⅓ cup (80 ml) in a spray bottle, to be kept warm in the bain-marie, and ⅔ cup (160 ml) at room temperature for the liebigs (a physically jellified emulsion).

For the Bitter Jelly. Remove the zest from half the grapefruit. Soak 2 gelatin leaves in cold water. Bring the spring water to a boil. Remove the water from the heat, and add the grapefruit zest and the gelatin. Cover tightly and leave to infuse for 20 minutes. Pour through a strainer and set aside at room temperature. Lay the very thin strips of bream on disks of lightly oiled parchment paper to form circles approximately 5 inches (12 cm) in diameter. Chill in the refrigerator.

For the Liebigs. Soak 2 gelatin leaves in cold water. Warm up a scant cup (200 ml) of Couhins wine and add the gelatin leaves. Season well. Put the mixture in a small bowl, place in another bowl filled with crushed ice. Leave the jelly to set. Emulsify the jelly in a blender by gradually pouring in the ⅔ cup (160 ml) of flavored olive oil. Divide the liebig mixture evenly among 6 large bowls. Place in the refrigerator to let the liebigs set.

Pour the bitter jelly, which should be very fluid in consistency, over the liebigs. Gently lay the disks of bream on top. Spray each bream ring with the warm olive oil, and add a pinch of fleur de sel and one twist of the pepper mill. Serve immediately.

Château Couhins blanc 2005

Very fragrant and subtle, this white wine's vivacity and freshness are the ideal accompaniment to this fine and delicate fish. Its round, refined character marries well with the fish, which is prepared to be both tender and crisp. The iodine, citrus, and spicy notes balance with the flavor of the dish.

—Patrick Borras, Sommelier

Château Couhins-Lurton

The same estate as Château Couhins until it was split off in 1968, this is a property that would have disappeared from view if not for the intervention of André Lurton. The 19th-century château has been restored and a new cellar added, and the estate's pure Sauvignon Blanc white continues to win praise for its finesse and ability to age.

In the battle to prevent the complete urbanization of the historical vineyards of the Northern Graves, the name of André Lurton stands out. The instigator of the appellation Pessac-Léognan (1987), which covers this area, and the president of its winegrowers association for nearly 20 years, Lurton has also come to the rescue of a number of properties in peril—not least Château La Louvière and, of course, *Cru Classé* Château Couhins-Lurton.

The early history of this estate mirrors that of Château Couhins; the two were one and the same until they were divided in 1968. Initially renowned for its red wines, its white wines were first referred to in the 1898 edition of Cocks & Féret, when Couhins was producing an average 10 tonneaux (the equivalent of 12,000 bottles). This had risen to 25 tonneaux (30,000 bottles) by the 1940s under the ownership of the Hanappier and Gasqueton families, surpassing the 12 tonneaux (14,400 bottles) of red. Before 1950 it was occasionally bottled under the name Château Cantebau.

The reputation and price of the white wine (around 60,000 old French Francs per tonneau at the time) led to its classification in 1959, but by the late 1960s the estate was a shadow of its former self. Apparently the owner, Madame Gasqueton (also owner of Château Calon-Ségur in Saint-Estèphe), was considering uprooting the vines. Michel Delon of Château Léoville Las Cases, a family friend and adviser, was made aware of this and contacted André Lurton to see if anything could be done.

Lurton agreed to lease the vineyard and, despite its deplorable state (missing wires and stakes and badly pruned vines) and limited plantings (a couple of hectares), produced his first white wine here in 1967. Unfortunately, 1968, like 1963 and 1965, proved another lamentable vintage and the Gasqueton family finally decided to sell the estate. The bulk of the land was acquired by the Institut National de la Recherche Agronomique (INRA), along with the title Château Couhins; the château and cellars were purchased by a local pharmacist.

Though INRA honored the rental agreement with Lurton through 1978, in 1972 it sold him a 1.5-hectare parcel of vines, thus dividing the estate and launching the cru Couhins-Lurton. In 1992 Lurton was able to buy the 19th-century château, with its splendid park designed by the noted landscape designer Lebreton, as well as the cellars. Renovation started in 1998;

the château underwent restoration while the old cellars were dismantled and the stones used to build a new cellar and repair other buildings.

Today, Couhins-Lurton *blanc* comprises nearly 6 hectares of gravel and sandy-gravel soils on a limestone bedrock planted entirely to Sauvignon Blanc. There are two principal parcels, one on top of a slope near the château and the other lower down, beyond the cellars of neighboring Château Couhins, near Château Pont de Langon.

Until the new cellar was operational in 2001 the wine was made at La Louvière. The procedure remains the same: the hand-picked grapes are fermented and the wines aged for ten months in oak *barriques*. These are predominantly Vosges oak barrels made by a Burgundian cooper and approximately 50 percent are renewed each year. A recent innovation initiated

Château Couhins-Lurton

was better known for its reds. Just over 17 hectares of Merlot and Cabernet Sauvignon were planted in the early 1990s a few miles away near Château de Rochemorin, another Lurton estate. The grapes were initially blended with other wines, but in 2002 the first vintage of Couhins-Lurton red was produced at the new cellar.

An unusually high percentage of Merlot (75 percent) is used in the blend and the wine aged in 75 percent new oak barrels. It is supple, round, and tender when young, with a spiciness provided by the fruit and oak and something of the smoky nature of the Graves. A tradition and name have been revived, albeit with a newly fashioned vineyard.

in 2003 was bottling half the yearly production with a screwcap closure, the rest with traditional cork.

The wine, which has great vivacity in youth, also has a remarkable and somewhat surprising capacity to age. Delicious at three to four years with a lemony persistence and crisp acidity that gives line and length, it gradually fills out on the palate, gaining a mineral, nutty complexity while at the same time preserving the fruit and zesty freshness. Top vintages can age upwards of 20 years, making this pure Sauvignon Blanc a somewhat exceptional wine.

André Lurton has also concerned himself with the creation of a red Couhins-Lurton, a throwback to the 19th century, when Couhins

Above:
André Lurton,
owner of the estate.
Opposite:
The barrel cellars at
Château Couhins-Lurton
welcomed their first
harvests in 2001.
Following pages:
The grounds of Château
Couhins-Lurton, created in
the late 19th century based
on plans by the celebrated
landscape designer
Lebreton.

Georges Blanc

Asparagus Chartreuse with Spider Crab and Caviar

For the Chartreuses. Gently peel the green asparagus with a vegetable peeler and chop into pieces 3 inches (8 cm) long. Add the asparagus to a pan of boiling salted water for about 4 minutes: it should be cooked but still have some bite. Immediately cool the asparagus down in a bowl of iced water to stop the cooking process and keep its wonderful color; do not leave the asparagus in the iced water for too long. Drain and set aside.

Peel the white asparagus and slice with a mandoline or vegetable peeler into thin strips. Place into boiling salted water for 30 seconds, and then cool down immediately in iced water.

Mix the spider-crab meat with the mayonnaise and lemon juice. The quantities are important for the consistency: the rillettes mixture should be creamy, but without any excess sauce. Season to taste.

Gently slice the green asparagus spears in half lengthwise. Line rings approximately 2 ½ inches (6 cm) in diameter with the sliced asparagus spears, arranged diagonally. Fill each ring with spider-crab meat and top with as much caviar as you would like.

For the Shellfish Oil. Whisk together the grapeseed oil with the shellfish carcass jus reduction (or reduced lobster bisque, if using).

Turn out a vegetable chartreuse in the center of each plate. Place the white asparagus strips evenly around the sides of the chartreuses. Dribble the shellfish oil around each chartreuse or decorate with crayfish butter and a dash of balsamic vinegar. Serve immediately.

Ingredients
Serves 4

For the Chartreuses
- 75 small green asparagus
- 45 white asparagus
- 1 pound (450 g) shelled spider-crab meat*
- ½ cup (150 ml) mayonnaise
- ¾ juice of 1 lemon
- 3 ¼ ounces (90 g) caviar
- Salt and freshly ground pepper

For the Shellfish Oil
- 3 tablespoons grapeseed oil
- 3 tablespoons shellfish carcass jus reduction (langoustines, prawns, crabs, etc.) or lobster bisque reduced by half, which you then add to the grapeseed oil

*I love spider crab for its wonderful character and iodine flavor, but you can also use shelled edible crab. Whichever you use, make sure the crabmeat is as fresh as possible.

Recipe from *Fêtes des saveurs* by Georges Blanc, Hachette Pratique, Paris, 2004.

Château Couhins-Lurton blanc 2004

Pale yellow, crystal, and brilliant—the fresh, clean nose reveals white fruit and citrus such as pear and lemon. Entry on the palate is clean, fresh, and round. A rich finish with just a hint of fennel and cardamom to lend finesse and elegance. An exquisite, immediate *vin de plaisir* from a classic vintage year. Serve this wine at 51-53°F (11-12°C). There's no need to decant: let the wine rest in the bottle, and its clean aromas will soon find you.

Pairing wine with asparagus has always been a sommelier's challenge. Here, I have found a wonderful combination of the spider crab's iodine, the saline notes of caviar, and the delicate flavor of asparagus. To my mind, this is without a doubt one of the greatest signature dishes from Georges Blanc, who has a remarkable talent for showcasing each ingredient.

I love the clarity of this wine, which gives a new dimension to the dish without compromising its own personality.

—Fabrice Sommier, Sommelier

Château de Fieuzal

The wheel continues on its inexorable course. Already a cutting-edge estate in the 1980s, Château de Fieuzal is enjoying a revival today. Irish ownership and a motivated new team are providing the momentum, and the wines—both red and white— have reclaimed the rich, full-bodied assertiveness that first brought them to our attention.

Château de Fieuzal is a centuries-old property set in the heart of the Graves region, the historic cradle of Bordeaux wines. Its beginnings can be traced back to the 16th century, when the first parcels of land on the estate belonged to Jean and François Garderes, laborers at the neighboring *seigneurie*. After passing through the hands of the Bordeaux Dabadie family, the château returned to the Fieuzal family in the 17th century through marriage and inheritance.

In 1851, on the death of Lovely Fieuzal, the last descendant of the name, the property was made up of the Fieuzal and Haut-Gardère lands. The estate was then bought by Pierre Louis Eugène and Louis Armand Alfred de Griffon, whose wife was a member of the eminent La Rochefoucauld family. In 1864 the land was divided between the two brothers:

one part became Château Haut-Gardère and the other Château de Fieuzal.

In 1892 Fieuzal was bought by Jean Ricard, then owner of Domaine de Chevalier and Château Malartic-Lagravière. It was his ambition to enhance the reputation and quality of the château's wines, and he thus opened the first chapter of Fieuzal's great wine-making history. His son Abel succeeded him in 1908. On Abel's death in 1945, his daughter Odette and Swedish son-in-law, Erik Bocké, took over the estate. A remarkable character for the time, Bocké was the man behind the development of Fieuzal white wine. Produced initially in tiny quantities, the wine was not put forward for classification until 1953. Château de Fieuzal's red wine is, however, one of the *Crus Classés* of Graves.

Nature, lady
of the house at Fieuzal.

From pruning the vine to harvesting the grapes, everything contributes to the purity of the wines.

In 1974 chemist Georges Négrevergne acquired the property and appointed his son-in-law, Gérard Gribelin, to the helm of the 15-hectare estate. Gribelin and his talented technical director, Michel Dupuy, were true wine-making pioneers for both red and white. They renovated the barrel cellars and installed heat-regulated stainless steel vats, which help prolong the maceration time for red wines and preserve the aromatic potential of the white musts. They increased the number of new barrels and lengthened the amount of time for aging the white wines on lees. This period also saw the emergence of a second wine, L'Abeille de Fieuzal, which allowed the winemaker to refine the wine selected for use in the *grand vin*. The 1980s marked a turning point in the château's history, a period when the winery

acquired the cutting-edge technical know-how to produce rich, powerful red wines and fat, extremely fresh white wines. The Château de Fieuzal 1985 white is still a classic today. Characterized by brioche aromas, it has a delicately fresh, generous, and well-balanced palate.

By replanting and making new acquisitions, the owners increased the property to 45 hectares by the early 1990s, adding further prestige to the Fieuzal name. In 1994 the Négrevergne family sold the estate to the Banque Populaire financial group, which one year later bought the neighboring Château Haut-Gardère and re-created the original estate.

A new era began in 2001 with the arrival of Brenda and Lochlann Quinn, an epicurean

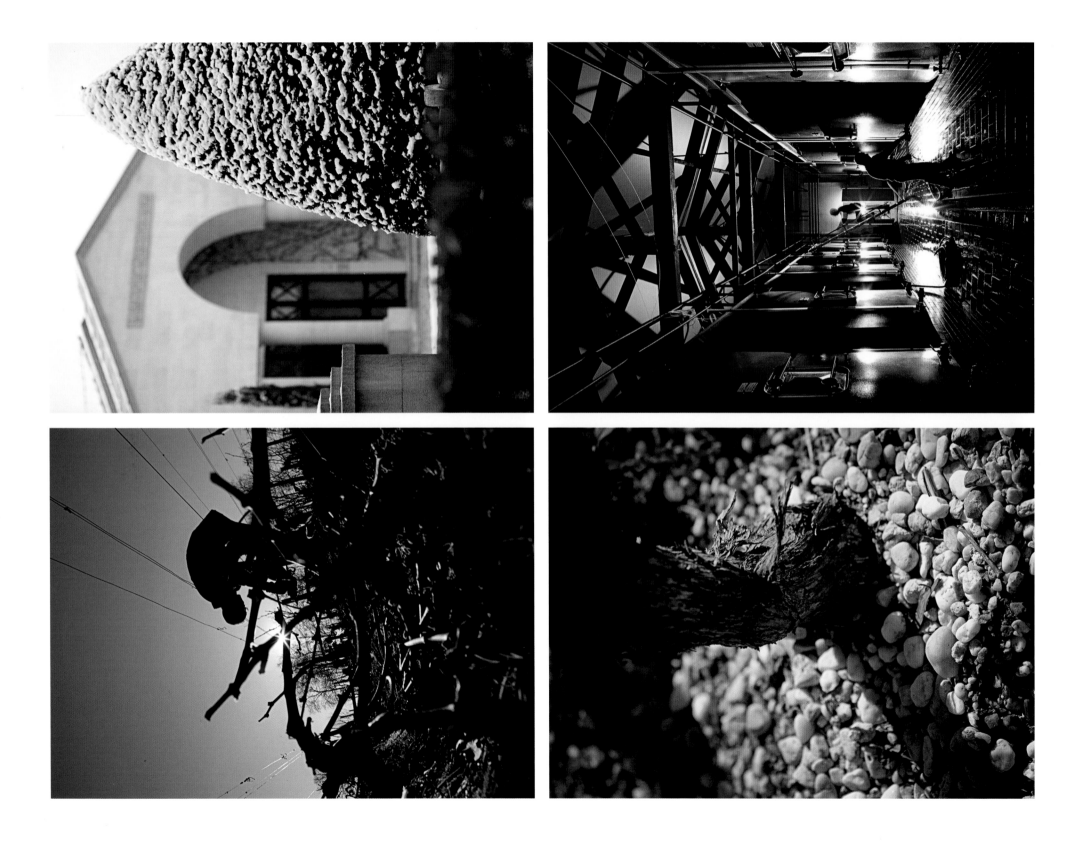

Irish couple who took over the estate. Passionate aficionados of French wine, they made it their duty to uphold and develop the unique character of the place by preserving the typicity and authenticity of its wines.

Today the vineyard stretches over 75 hectares, 10 of which are dedicated to white grape varieties. The Château de Fieuzal terrain is principally made up of sandy gravel with clay and limestone. The Cabernet Sauvignon, Merlot, Cabernet Franc, and Petit Verdot vines are planted in poor, deep, gravelly soil, which offers excellent drainage to the vine stocks. The Sauvignon Blanc, Sémillon, and Muscadelle varieties are located on gravel and limestone hilltops, a type of soil that preserves the freshness and bouquet of the white wines.

The impetus provided by the Quinns will soon enter its next phase with plans to renovate the barrel cellars and fermenting room, the start of a new era that promises to take Château de Fieuzal even farther along the path of finesse and excellence.

Below:
Lochlann Quinn.
Opposite:
Last light on a winter's day.

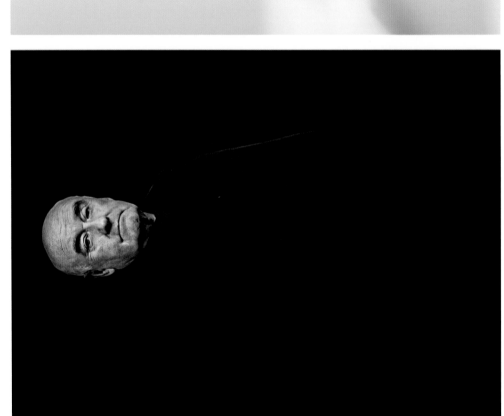

Patrick Guilbaud

Fillet of Venison Poached in Sweet Spices with Soft Polenta and Muesli Clusters

For the Grand Veneur Sauce. Make a bouquet garni with thyme, juniper, whole cloves, peppercorns, and bay leaf. Make a marinade by cutting the vegetables in a large mirepoix and then sweating them in some oil until slightly softened. Lightly crush the garlic and add it, along with the bouquet garni, toward the end of the cooking. Pour in the wine and bring to a simmer. Remove the pan from the heat and transfer the contents to a suitable nonreactive container. When the mixture has cooled, break up the bones and add them to the vegetables. Leave them to marinate for 2 days. The day before you plan to serve the dish, strain the mixture and separate the bones and vegetables. In a wide casserole, sear the bones and the trimmings in more oil until lightly browned and then add the vegetables. Sprinkle lightly with flour and let cook briefly in the fat to remove any rawness. Deglaze the casserole with the previously strained wine followed by the game stock. Simmer for 4 hours on low heat, skimming regularly. Strain the liquid and reduce by half, or until a full flavor is achieved. Finish the sauce by adding a mixture of crème fraîche, red currant jam, and a drop of cognac and then return to a gentle simmer. If the sauce has not reached a nap consistency, thicken slightly with a slurry made with potato flour (or arrowroot). Season very well with salt and pepper, and set aside.

For the Polenta. Melt the butter in the milk. Add the polenta and cook on low heat. Then, fold in the crème fraîche. Pour into small rectangular 3 x 1-inch (8 x 3 cm) molds. Leave to cool, turn out, and cut in half lengthwise. Coat the cooked polenta in uncooked polenta. Set aside.

For the Balsamic Nib Syrup. Combine all the ingredients in a sauteuse pan and reduce until you obtain a syrup consistency.

For the Muesli Clusters. Mix together the muesli and the dried fruit, chopped into small pieces. Make a light caramel with the superfine sugar. Roll the fruit and muesli in the caramel.

Poach the fillets of venison in spiced red wine (made by infusing port with juniper berries, cinnamon stick, orange and lemon peel, and pepper for about 8 minutes). Heat up the polenta under the grill. Roll the venison in the grand veneur sauce. Steam the Brussels sprout petals.

Dress each plate with a line of balsamic nib syrup using a brush. Now arrange the polenta, Brussels sprout petals, and kumquats. Complete each plate with a poached venison steak. Decorate with the muesli clusters. Serve immediately.

Ingredients
Serves 4

- 4 venison steaks, 5 ¼ ounces (150 g) each
- 12 Brussels sprout petals
- 2 preserved kumquats

For the Grand Veneur Sauce
- 3 onions
- 3 carrots
- 4 celery stalks
- 1 garlic bulb
- 4 thyme sprigs
- 10 juniper berries
- 4 whole cloves
- 20 whole black peppercorns
- 1 bay leaf
- 11 pounds (5 kg) venison bones
- 3 quarts (3 liters) game stock
- 4 quarts (4 liters) red wine
- Oil
- All-purpose flour
- Crème fraîche
- Red currant jam
- Cognac
- Potato flour
- Salt and freshly ground pepper

For the Polenta
- 1 quart (1 liter) whole milk
- ⅔ cup (150 g) unsalted butter
- 1 cup (150 g) fine polenta
- ¼ cup (40 ml) crème fraîche

For the Balsamic Nib Syrup
- ½ cup (100 g) sugar
- 1 quart (1 liter) balsamic vinegar
- 10 ½ ounces (300 g) cocoa nibs

For the Muesli Clusters
- ⅔ cup (80 g) muesli
- 2 ½ tablespoons (40 g) superfine sugar
- 1 ¾ ounces (50 g) dried fruit

Château de Fieuzal 2000

For this recipe I chose a Château de Fieuzal 2000: a wine of great class with ripe red fruit and sweet spice aromas. Its flattering, concentrated palate balanced by smooth tannins marries perfectly with this subtly spiced dish of rich, powerful, and velvety flavors.

—Yohann Pinol, Sommelier

Château Haut-Bailly

Elegance and balance: these are the bywords for the red wine of this estate. Its foundations are a vineyard that has remained constant for nearly 400 years and the will of the owners to maintain a continuity of style. With 21st-century fine tuning added to the mix, Haut-Bailly has never been as pure and precise.

Preceding pages:
Built in 1872, the current Château stands on a vineyard that dates back several centuries.

Above:
The barrel cellars walls are made of Haut-Bailly's shelly sandstone.

Old vines on an enchanting ridge.

There is something reassuringly enduring about Château Haut-Bailly. The property is deep-rooted, its aura one of family commitment and strength, while the style of the wine remains unequivocally devoted to elegance and length. Change has occurred, and for the better, but continuity remains the objective at this estimable estate.

The property is set on one of the highest ridges in the commune of Léognan. The surface area of 33 hectares has barely altered over the last four centuries; currently 30 hectares are planted to a density of 10,000 vines per hectare. The bulk of the property, which only produces red wine, is planted with Cabernet Sauvignon (64 percent) with a complement of Merlot (30 percent) and Cabernet Franc (6 percent). But there's also a 100-year-old parcel of mixed vines, including Carménère, Malbec, and Petit Verdot, which annually represent 20 percent of the blend.

The vine was cultivated at Pujau, a *lieu-dit* or place name on the gravel ridge, as far back as 1461. But the origins of the present vineyard date from around 1530, the planting initiated by two merchant families from the Basque country, the Goyanèches and the Daitzes.

The property was put on sound commercial footing in the 17th century by wine merchant Nicolas de Leuvarde and his brother-in-law, Firmin Le Bailly, a Parisian banker who gave his name to the estate. The property changed hands a number of times in the course of the 18th century until it was acquired by Christophe de Lafaurie, Baron de Monbadon (whose son, Laurent, would be elected mayor of Bordeaux in 1805).

In 1872 Haut-Bailly was purchased by Alcide Bellot des Minières, an engineer who had made his fortune with sugar, cotton, and tobacco plantations in Virginia. A colorful but committed man, he reorganized and enlarged the vineyard and constructed the present château.

Under his guidance the reputation of Haut-Bailly grew, and by the early part of the 20th century the wines were selling for the same price as Haut-Brion and the Médoc first growths. Following des Minières' death in 1906, his wife and daughter continued the succession but sold the property in 1918. It then changed hands several times before being purchased in 1955 by Belgian wine merchant Daniel Sanders.

The war years and the depression had inflicted their dues on Haut-Bailly, and by that time the vineyard had been reduced to 10 hectares. Haut-

Bailly regained some of its luster in the 1960s, when Daniel Sanders launched a program of replanting and renovation. In 1979 Daniel's son, Jean, took over direction of the estate and instituted a policy of severe selection, achieving quality and consistency at Haut-Bailly once again.

However, difficulties with joint ownership eventually forced him to sell, and in 1998 American banker Robert G. Wilmers and his wife, Elisabeth, entered the picture. The transition was seamless, with the Wilmers taking a direct hand in the management of the estate, supported by a talented and motivated team headed by Veronique Sanders, granddaughter of the former owner, with Gabriel Vialard responsible for wine-making.

The cellar harbours some legendary bottles.

From the vine to
the barrel cellars, rigour
and precision are crucial.

The changes have been well thought out and ultimately rewarding, with the wines gaining greater purity, precision, and texture since 2004. The vineyard was the first to receive attention. Soil analysis revealed a mosaic of soils, with the best parcels having 30 inches (75 centimeters) of gravel and then a compact, clay-based subsoil. The *cuvier* was then organized to allow for parcel-by-parcel vinification, and the number of small tanks quadrupled to 30. Finally, three barrel cellars were created on three different levels in the expanded winery.

Château Haut-Bailly still has a severe system of selection, with only 50 percent of the production going into the *grand vin*. Aging is in oak barrels, of which 50 to 65 percent are renewed

yearly. A third of the production is then destined for the second wine, La Parde de Haut-Bailly, and the rest for a generic appellation wine.

The unique terroir at Haut-Bailly leaves its distinctive signature on the wines to guarantee exceptional constancy year after year. Strict selection and an approach to wine-making that is based on the search for balance and harmony help define the style. These are wines that combine finesse and concentration, suppleness and structure, as well as aromatic complexity and supple tannins.

It's been a quiet revolution, as one would expect. Haut-Bailly has been modernized, but its values remain intact.

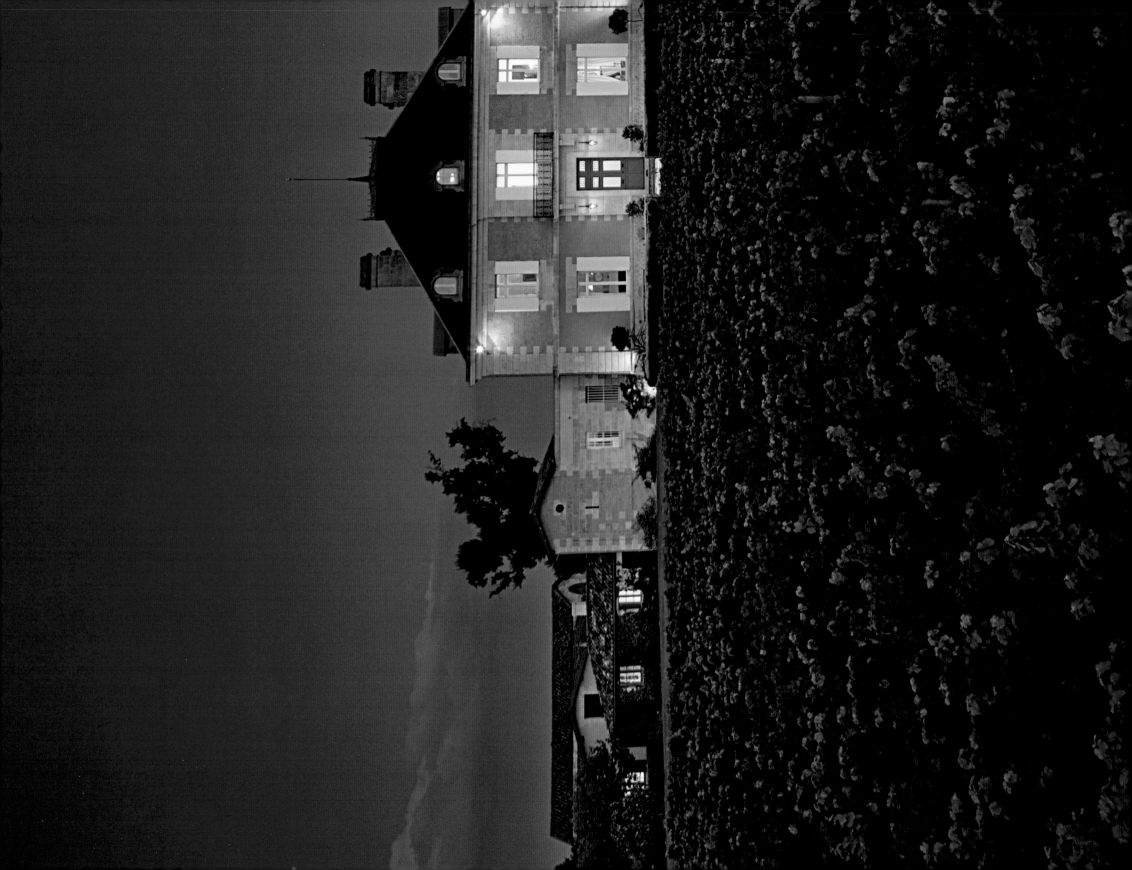

Peter Goossens
Anjou Pigeon with Jerusalem Artichoke, Sweet Corn, and Salsifies

Ask your butcher to remove the pigeon breasts for you, but take the carcasses home, too.

For the Salsifies. Peel the salsifies and cut into 1-inch-long (3 cm) pieces. Cook them in boiling salted water for 1 hour and strain. Brown the pieces of salsify in a knob of butter. Keep warm.

For the Sauce. Pan-fry the carcasses in butter until they are nicely browned. Add the shallot and garlic and sauté until softened, and then deglaze with the cognac. Pour in the chicken stock. Season with the thyme and bay leaf. Reduce the sauce for 30 minutes. Remove the carcasses, strain the juices. Add the juices to a pan and reduce. Finish the sauce with butter. Keep the sauce to one side.

For the Vegetables. Sauté the sweet corn in a knob of butter. Blanch the Brussels sprouts and quarter them. Sauté them in a knob of butter. Clean the chanterelles and sauté in butter. Peel and cook the onions. Quarter them and cook and reduce in the brown stock. Keep all the vegetables warm.

Peel the Jerusalem artichokes, cut them into cubes, and cook for 20 minutes in equal measures of water and milk. Drain and process them in a blender to obtain a smooth purée. Combine with the crème fraîche and keep warm.

Peel and finely slice the shallot crosswise. Dip the shallot rings in milk and then in flour. Deep-fry the battered shallot rings at 300°F (150°C). Set aside.

For the Pigeon. Pan-fry the pigeon breasts for 20 minutes in 2 ½ tablespoons (40 g) of butter, turning regularly. Add the cooked lardons. Keep warm.

Decorate four dinner plates with small drops of black currant coulis. Arrange the pigeon breasts on the plates. Sprinkle with a few crushed cocoa beans. Add the fried shallot rings. Heat up the sauce, adding a few sage leaves and a knob of butter. Sauce the plates. Serve immediately.

Ingredients
Serves 4

- 2 Anjou pigeons

- 3 ounces (80 g) salsifies
- ⅓ cup (80 g) unsalted butter

For the Sauce
- 1 shallot
- 1 garlic clove
- 3 tablespoons cognac
- 1 quart (1 liter) chicken stock
- 1 thyme sprig
- 1 bay leaf
- 3 sage leaves
- 4 teaspoons (20 g) unsalted butter

For the Vegetables
- 1 ounce (30 g) sweet corn
- 1 ¾ ounces (50 g) Brussels sprouts
- 3 ½ ounces (100 g) chanterelle mushrooms
- 2 ounces (60 g) pickling onions
- ⅔ cup (150 ml) brown stock made from bouillon powder or cube
- 1 ½ ounces (45 g) Jerusalem artichokes
- 2 cups (500 ml) whole milk
- ½ cup (100 ml) crème fraîche
- 1 shallot

- ½ cup (50 g) lardons (cooked)
- 1 teaspoon black currant coulis
- 3 cocoa beans
- All-purpose flour
- Peanut oil

Château Haut-Bailly 2005

Powerful, elegant Cabernet Sauvignon and pigeon is a classic pairing—and for good reason. The silky character of the Haut-Bailly Cabernets is the ideal match for the structure and flavor of pigeon. The bird is cooked at a low temperature, a process that ensures the meat retains its juices. But it also helps to have a wine that holds a lot of fruit. A 2005 Haut-Bailly is ideal for our purposes. The wine's spicy aroma balances with the pigeon's succulence and concentration. The dense, tight tannins tell us that we can expect great class and longevity in this Haut-Bailly from such a legendary vintage year. It is superb with the crispy pigeon skin and the corn.

—Soen Martijn, Sommelier

Château
La Mission Haut-Brion

Powerful and concentrated, with a lushness of fruit and force of tannin, La Mission is the antithesis of its stablemate, Haut-Brion, across the road. An independent character from its early 16th-century origins, La Mission has nonetheless benefited from the care, attention, and expertise lavished by the Dillon family since 1983.

Château La Mission Haut-Brion lies across the road from Château Haut-Brion, its neighbor in the precincts of Bordeaux. The two venerable estates have much in common, not least the Haut-Brion designation and since 1983 a shared ownership and wine-making team. Despite appearances, though, these are two distinct properties, La Mission with its own history, terroir, and character.

The majority of La Mission's vineyard lies in the suburb of Talence, although a couple of parcels are intermixed with the Haut-Brion vines in nearby Pessac. About a third of the vineyard surrounds the château and cellars, the rest extending down toward the university campus but separated from the "home base" by the Bordeaux–to–Arcachon railway line.

In recent years the vineyard has been steadily replanted and expanded. Just over two hectares were recouped from Laville Haut-Brion in 1990 and the vineyard that was formerly Château La Tour Haut-Brion (5.05 hectares) was incorporated in 2006. All told, this has brought La Mission's vineyard to a total of 26.5 hectares.

The land is generally flatter, more plateaulike, than that found at Haut-Brion, where there's a semblance of a *coteau*. The soil is also slightly richer, still gravelly but with a little more clay and a subsoil that is chalky sand. This has

Preceding pages:
In the midst of the French garden, Bacchus greets visitors to La Mission.
Below:
The front view of La Mission Haut-Brion, with its cloister and 17th-century chapel.
Opposite:
The cloister.

Opposite:
Notre-Dame d'Aubrion,
consecrated in 1698.

Following pages,
bottom left:
Detail of the chapel's
stained-glass windows,
some of which date from
the 16th century.
Right:
The Grand Chai
(main barrel cellar).

Château La Mission Haut-Brion

permitted a higher density of planting than at Haut-Brion, with La Mission planted to 10,000 vines per hectare.

Does this help explain the divergence in style? The blend of grape varieties seems unable to provide the answer, for La Mission's vineyard is planted to 43 percent Merlot, 47 percent Cabernet Sauvignon, and 10 percent Cabernet Franc, similar to Haut-Brion. There's also the same penchant for Merlot, with 55 percent the average in the final blend for both wines.

Trying to explain the difference in style is more difficult than experiencing it. If Haut-Brion is about elegance, finesse, and polished texture, then La Mission represents power and concentration with a lushness of fruit and force of tannin that gives it a florid, "masculine" quality. This is very much the case in exceptional years (1929, 1955, 1959, 1961, 1978,

1982, 1989, 1990, 2000, 2005), although La Mission maintains consistency in lesser vintages as well. Aging potential is at least 30 to 40 years.

The origins of La Mission date back to 1540 and the sale by Louis de Rostaing, *seigneur* of La Tour, of a parcel of vines, known as Arrejedhuys, to a well-to-do merchant named Arnaut de Lestonnac. During the same period Arnaut's brother-in-law, Jean de Pontac, was in the throes of developing Haut-Brion, so it seems probable that he had similar designs for the parcel to become the base around which La Mission was built.

Arnaut's son, Pierre, succeeded his father and built a house and cellars on the land. The property then fell to his daughter, Olive de Lestonnac, the future *Dame* of Margaux. A wealthy and pious lady, she eventually bequeathed the 9-hectare estate

Château La Mission Haut-Brion

Following pages:
The rising sun barely dispels
the winter morning mist.

to the church in 1650, but it was not until 1664 that her heirs handed it over to the religious authorities, who in turn transferred it to Lazarite priests, also known as the Congregation de la Mission. It seems clear that the name originated here.

The Lazarite fathers further improved the property, building a chapel, which was consecrated in 1698, and the château at the beginning of the 18th century. The wine was appreciated by the Duc de Richelieu, governor of Guyenne (1755), and his successor, Maréchal Duc de Mouchy, who introduced it to the French court.

Like all religious assets, La Mission, then 15 hectares, was confiscated by the state during the Revolution and in 1792 sold to Martial-Victor Vaillant for 302,000 livres in paper money, considered a significant sum at the time. The property stayed with the Vaillant family

until 1821, when it was sold to Célestin Chiapella.

Chiapella hailed from New Orleans and he and his son, Jérôme, played an important role in the evolution of La Mission. They established the name, improved the vineyard, and enclosed the property, constructing the iron gate that is still in use today. Their business contacts helped establish markets in the United States and Great Britain, and by 1860 the wine was selling at the same price as the Médoc second growths. A model boat, commissioned by Chiapella and once used as a weather vane, commemorates the transatlantic connection.

La Mission was again sold in 1884 and there followed a number of owners including Victor Coustau, in 1903, who later sold to his friend Frédéric Woltner in 1919. The property by then was in a jaded state and it was the Woltners,

131

in particular Frédéric's son, Henri, who put La Mission back on the map. Revolutionary glass-lined steel fermentation vats were introduced, for better temperature control and hygiene, while the vineyard was replanted and improved.

Unfortunately, the later part of the Woltner era was less glorious. Investment became limited to the extent that new oak barrels were not even purchased. This was the situation when the Dillon family of Château Haut-Brion acquired the property in 1983.

Since then, of course, there have been sweeping changes. The château and chapel were renovated in 2000, while the garden with its neat rows of box hedges continues to be kept in immaculate condition. A new stainless steel *cuvier* was built in 1987, and more recently (in 2006) the *chai* was completely redesigned to include new barrel cellars (80 percent of the barrels are renewed each year) and bottling and storage areas. A cloister for visitor reception has also seen the light of day. The vineyard continues to be cultivated with all due care and attention.

Changes have indeed been made and consistency improved, but La Mission retains the inherent forceful character it has displayed over the centuries. The terroir, if puzzling, is clearly exceptional, for it is the one constant factor at this outstanding domaine.

Alain Passard

Autumn Red Beet in a Guérande Gray Salt Crust

Scour a kitchen garden or local market for a lovely-looking beet, farmed naturally with the expertise of a true gardener. Choose one weighing around 14 ounces (400 g).

Gently clean the beet with a soft brush under cold running water and remove any remnants of dirt. On a baking tray, form a very thick layer of gray sea salt to create a secure base for the beet and then bury the vegetable under a pyramid of the sea salt. The beet must be completely covered, so be generous with the salt.

Preheat the oven to 275°F (140°C). Place the salt-crusted beet in the oven and cook for 2 hours. When done, leave the beet to cool down in its crust for 40 minutes.

In front of your guests, break through the salt crust, remove the beet whole, and cut lengthwise into 4 equal aiguillettes (long strips). Serve on warm plates with butter, melted and infused with the finely chopped fresh herbs. For a final touch, give a twist of the pepper mill over the warm beet strips just before eating. Don't forget the skin: it's the best part!

Ingredients
Serves 4

- 1 large red beet about 14 ounces (400 g), preferably Red Crapaudine*
- 4 ½ pounds (2 kg) gray sea salt (naturally rich in magnesium), preferably hand-harvested from Guérande
- 3 ½ tablespoons (50 g) unsalted butter
- 1 bunch fresh herbs (preferably chervil, tarragon, parsley, and coriander)
- Ground pepper

*Red Crapaudine: What's great about this variety of beet is its very sweet flavor, tender texture, and earthy fragrance. Its elongated shape makes it ideal for creating aiguillettes.

Château La Mission Haut-Brion rouge 2000

This wine has an elegant body with garnet highlights and an agreeably fine nose with dark fruit and cocoa notes. Equally elegant on the palate, it delivers a wonderful sweetness. Well-balanced and succulent, the tannins are supple but powerful. This red is also pleasantly fresh and lively, with a particularly graceful finish. It is a clean, precise, harmonious, and supremely refined wine— elegant through and through.

The earthy tones of the red beet are an interesting pairing with this great wine. The vegetable's subtle flavors perfectly balance the wine's sweetness and finesse, and the wine's freshness provides a lovely contrast to the dish.

—Guillaume Muller, Sommelier

Château
La Tour Haut-Brion

A "mystery" cru of changeable style but long and noble pedigree, La Tour Haut-Brion produced its last vintage in 2005. From firm and tannic to supple and approachable, it was at one time considered the second wine of La Mission Haut-Brion and has now been absorbed into that venerable estate.

Oposite, top:
Pascal Baratié, Vineyard
Manager at the estate.
Opposite, bottom:
H.R.H. Prince Robert
of Luxembourg.

Château La Tour Haut-Brion is now a fond memory of our past. The last vintage was produced in 2005 and since then the 5.05-hectare vineyard has been amalgamated with Château La Mission Haut-Brion. In terms of character and style La Tour was always a bit of a "mystery" *cru*, one could even say a chameleon, in part due to its limited production. But the pedigree was solid, as the history books recount.

From the Middle Ages to the Revolution La Tour Haut-Brion was part of the estate of the noble house of La Tour de Rostaing, sometimes called La Tour d'Esquivens, based in the parish of Talence. While most of the land at that time was in the hands of the church, the Rostaing family became one of the first lay producers to

make a quality wine. In 1540 Louis de Rostaing, *seigneur* of La Tour, also owned parcels of vines that later helped model La Mission Haut-Brion.

In the mid-18th century La Tour was still part of the noble house, now owned by the Saige family, wealthy and influential merchants who were also important landowners in the Graves. François-Armand Saige was mayor of Bordeaux from 1791 to 1793 before being condemned to the guillotine by a revolutionary committee.

One of the earliest references to the domaine under its full title of La Tour Haut-Brion is in the first edition (1850) of the Cocks & Féret guide to the wines of Bordeaux. The estate, we are informed, produced 25 tonneaux (the equivalent

of 30,000 bottles) of red wine and was owned by Jérôme and Joseph Cayrou. The brothers had bought the 7-hectare property in 1841 and it was probably they who appended the name Haut-Brion to that of La Tour.

The existing manor house, now a retirement home, was rebuilt by Louis Uzac, the owner from 1858 to 1884. He also restored the small two-story hexagonal tower adjacent to it that serves as a reminder of the origin of the vineyard's name.

At the turn of the 20th century La Tour Haut-Brion and La Mission Haut-Brion came under the same ownership when Victor Coustau acquired La Tour in 1890 and La Mission in 1903. It was from this date that La Tour started to be produced at La Mission. This arrangement continued after the sale of La Mission to Frédéric Woltner in 1919 and the death of Victor Coustau

in 1923. La Tour was eventually bequeathed to the Woltners in 1935 and the wine continued to be made at La Mission right up to the last vintage in 2005.

The Woltner period set a seal on the style of wine during the 20th century. La Tour was treated as the second wine of La Mission Haut-Brion; in terms of wine-making it had plenty of extraction and a fair portion of La Mission's *vin de presse* in the blend. The result was a deep-colored, firm, tannic, muscular wine with a reputation for being difficult when young but evolving well over a long period of time.

In 1983 the Woltner properties, including La Tour Haut-Brion, were sold to the Dillon family, owners of Château Haut-Brion. The change in the style of the wine was immediate, with the 1983 showing the way toward a more supple, approachable La Tour. This was partly due to a change in wine-making techniques and partly, as the decade came to a close, due to the increased percentage of young vines. By 1987 two-thirds of the vineyard had been replanted.

Indeed, the new management made a conscious decision to re-create the identity of La Tour. It was no longer to be considered the second wine of La Mission (La Chapelle de La Mission Haut-Brion was created for this purpose in 1991), and only wines from La Tour's vineyard were to be used to make the wine.

The replanting continued when two further parcels were renewed in 2000 and 2002. This led to a field planting of 34 percent Merlot, 22 percent Cabernet Franc and 44 percent Cabernet Sauvignon. The blends in more recent vintages, however, vary considerably; hence the fluctuation in styles. Compare the round and mellow 2000 (50 percent Merlot, 25 percent Cabernet

Franc, 25 percent Cabernet Sauvignon) to the fragrant, long, and linear 2005 (32 percent Merlot, 41 percent Cabernet Franc, 27 percent Cabernet Sauvignon).

This last vintage turned out to be the swan-song for Château La Tour Haut-Brion. Coming full circle, the vineyard has now been absorbed into the larger entity of Château La Mission Haut-Brion and the grapes from the young vineyard are being used at least initially for the second wine, La Chapelle de La Mission Haut-Brion.

Daniel Boulud
Crisp Paupiette of Sea Bass in a Barolo Sauce

For the Paupiette of Sea Bass. Make each fillet as rectangular as possible (about 5 x 2 inches [13 x 5 cm]) by trimming off uneven edges with a sharp knife. Salt and pepper the fillets and sprinkle them with 2 teaspoons of the chopped thyme. Using a knife, shape each potato lengthwise by cutting off the rounded outer flesh to form 4 rectangular pieces (do not cut off the tips of the potatoes). Cut each potato lengthwise into very thin, long slices with a vegetable slicer or mandoline. Each potato should yield about 16 slices (8 slices are needed to wrap each fish fillet). Do not rinse the potato slices as their starch will help the wrapped slices stick together. Toss the potato slices in 1 tablespoon (15 g) of the butter, melted, and a pinch of salt. Place a 10-inch (25-cm) square piece of parchment paper on the counter. Choose 8 potato slices of approximately the same length. Place a fillet of fish horizontally at the top of the parchment paper so you can match the length of the potato wrap to the length of the fish. Place the first slice of potato perpendicular to the fish starting on the left side. Place a second slice overlapping the first one about ⅜ inch (1 cm) from the left edge. Continue overlapping the potato slices until you have covered an area equal to the length of the fillet of fish. Center the fish horizontally in the middle of the potato wrap and fold the edges of the potatoes over the fish to enclose it entirely. Repeat the same process for the remaining fillets and refrigerate.

For the Leeks. Melt the butter in a sauté pan over medium heat. Add the leeks and sweat until soft, approximately 4 minutes. Season to taste with salt and pepper. Keep warm on the side.

For the Sauce. Heat the oil in a stockpot over high heat. Add the reserved sea bass bones, the shallots, mushrooms, and thyme sprig and cook for 8 to 10 minutes, stirring often. Add the chicken stock, bring to a boil, and cook until completely reduced. Add the Barolo wine, bring to a boil, and reduce by half. Remove and discard the fish bones with a mesh skimmer. Reduce the sauce to about 2 tablespoons (30 ml). Add the heavy cream, stir, and bring to a boil over low heat. Whisk in the butter, sugar, and salt and pepper to taste. Strain the sauce through a fine-mesh sieve and keep warm on the side. (If the sauce is too thick, add a little water to thin it.).

To cook the paupiettes, preheat the oven to 425°F (220°C). Melt the remaining 2 tablespoons (30 g) butter in a large nonstick sauté pan over high heat. Add the paupiettes and sauté until golden brown, 3 to 5 minutes on each side. If the fish is very thick, finish cooking in the oven for 4 to 5 minutes.

Place a bed of leeks in the middle of 4 warm plates and ladle the sauce around the leeks (about 2 tablespoons [30 ml] per plate). Place a paupiette on top of the leeks and garnish with half a sprig of thyme. Sprinkle the plate with minced chives.

Château La Tour Haut-Brion 2001

The 2001 La Tour Haut-Brion has a fine, delicate style that pairs wonderfully with the Paupiette of Sea Bass. It is medium-bodied and understated enough so as not to overpower this sophisticated fish. The red wine in the sauce elevates the dish and gives it enough depth and body to stand up to the wonderfully suave La Tour Haut-Brion.

—Daniel Johnnes, Sommelier

Ingredients
Serves 4

For the Paupiette of Sea Bass
- 4 sea bass fillets, approximately 7 ounces (200 g) each, skin removed, bones set aside for the sauce
- Salt and freshly ground black pepper
- 3 sprigs fresh thyme: 1 sprig, leaves only, chopped; 2 sprigs halved for garnish
- 2 very large baking potatoes, peeled
- 3 tablespoons (45 g) unsalted butter

For the Leeks
- 2 tablespoons (30 g) unsalted butter
- 2 leeks, white part only, thinly sliced
- Salt and freshly ground pepper

For the Sauce
- 1 tablespoon (15 ml) extra-virgin olive oil
- ½ cup (75 g) shallots, peeled and chopped
- ½ cup (35 g) white mushrooms, caps only, sliced
- ½ sprig fresh thyme
- 1 cup (24 cl) unsalted chicken stock
- 1 bottle (750 ml) of Barolo wine or other good red cooking wine
- 1 tablespoon (15 ml) heavy cream
- 8 tablespoons (1 stick) (120 g) unsalted butter
- Pinch of sugar
- Salt and freshly ground pepper
- 1 tablespoon minced chives

CHÂTEAU
LA TOUR HAUT-BRION
CRU CLASSE DE GRAVES
2001
DOMAINE CLARENCE DILLON S.A.
Propriétaire à Talence (Gironde) France
PESSAC-LEOGNAN
Appellation Pessac-Léognan Contrôlée
PRODUCE OF FRANCE
IS EN BOUTEILLE AU CHÂTEAU

Château Latour-Martillac

The Kressmann family has nurtured and developed Latour-Martillac since Alfred Kressmann acquired the property in 1929. His son Jean took over for about fifty years and now his grandsons, Tristan and Loïc, continue to oversee and fine-tune the estate's progress today, giving modern appeal to its classic red and white Graves.

The tower still exists, the last vestige of a 12th-century stronghold built by Montesquieu's forebears that controlled the route to Toulouse from the highest point in Martillac. The viticultural history of the domaine dates from the mid-19th century; plans from 1847 and 1860 attest to the fact that the vineyard was the estate's principal activity at that time.

In 1858 Edward Kressmann arrived from Germany, working first as a courtier in Bordeaux then as a *négociant* before establishing his own house in 1871. While prospecting for grapes and wine he discovered the quality and consistency of the white wines from the northern Graves, in particular those from the tiny vineyard of La Tour or Latour in Martillac.

The property at the time was little more than a farm with a 19th-century *chartreuse*, pasture, woods, and 12 hectares of clay-and-limestone soil on a southeast-facing slope planted principally to white grape varieties. Upon the death of the owner in 1929, Edward's son Alfred decided to buy La Tour, partly to secure the supply of wine and partly to keep it out of the hands of Eschenauer, a major rival and competitor who already owned the neighboring properties, Châteaux La Garde and Smith Haut Lafitte.

Alfred Kressmann created the wine we now know as Château Latour-Martillac. He devised the name and introduced the distinctive black and gold label. The 1934 vintage of the red, complete with new label, was served by the Wine and Spirit Benevolent Society to 700 guests at a coronation dinner in London to mark the accession of King George VI to the English throne. Alfred's son Jean was given the responsibility of managing the estate after the Second World War.

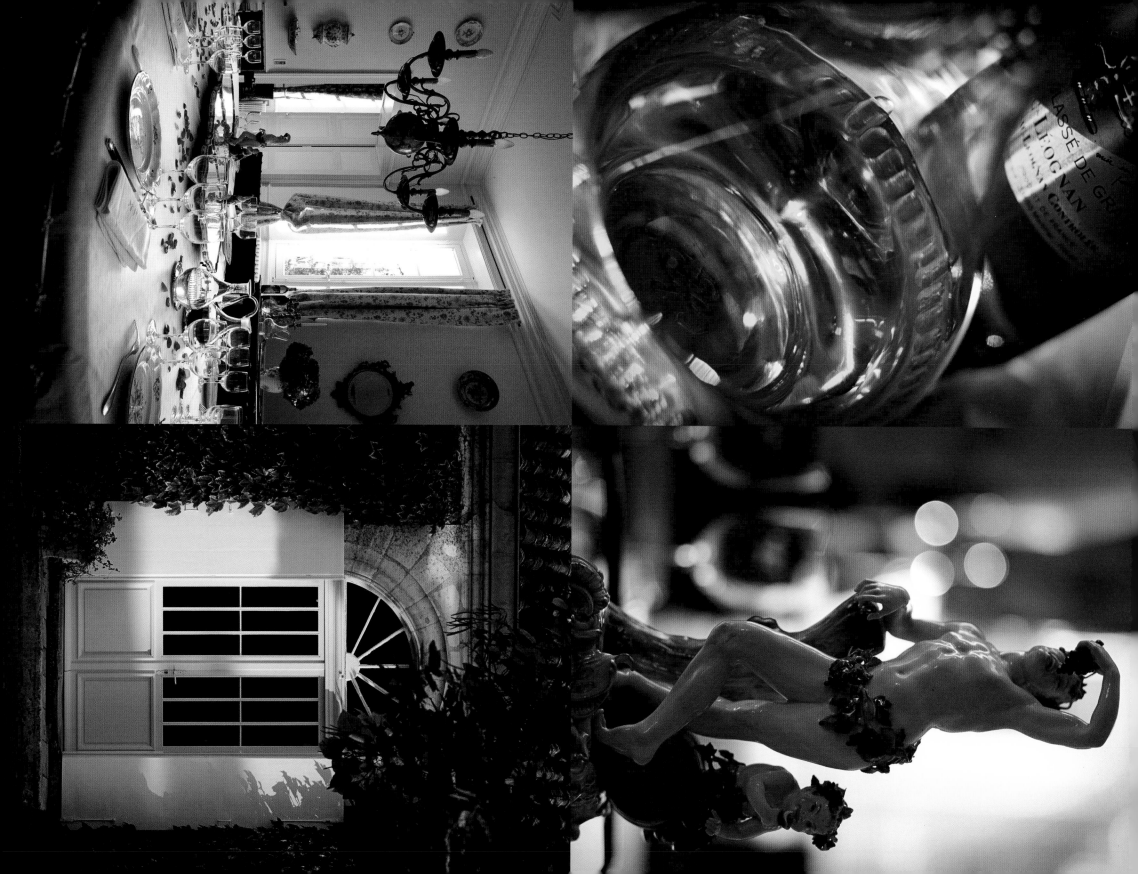

The estate was initially known for its white wines, although the red was the first to be classified, in 1953, the white following in 1959. Sémillon was the principal variety (there is still a tiny plot that was grafted in 1884) and remained conspicuously so through the late 1990s, providing the honeyed notes and creamy texture the wine achieves with age.

Recent vintages, though, have a higher percentage of Sauvignon Blanc (up to 60 percent, the rest Sémillon with a pinch of Muscadelle) and are more aromatic with citrus-grapefruit notes in youth. Whatever the blend, the wine is characterized by acidity and freshness, clearly influenced by the terroir.

Under the direction of Jean Kressmann, planting at the estate was increased in the 1950s, particularly after the destructive 1956 frost, then in the 1970s the area planted to red varieties

was further expanded. During this period about 10 hectares of land on the plateau close to the village of Martillac were secured and planted mainly with Cabernet Sauvignon, the dry, warm, gravelly soil being conducive to this variety.

Later in the 1990s there was further expansion of the vineyard with the acquisition of more land on the plateau and the cultivation of another plot further west. Cabernet Sauvignon and Merlot were the principal varieties planted, but there has also been a steady increase in Petit Verdot, which entered the blend for Latour-Martillac in 1997. All told the vineyard now totals 46 hectares, of which 36 are red (60 percent Cabernet Sauvignon, 35 percent Merlot, 5 percent Petit Verdot).

The late 1980s and early 1990s also saw a shake-up in management and changes on the technical side. Jean Kressmann's sons, Tristan

The red Latour-Martillac, which was classified in 1953, is an often understated wine with pleasing fruit, a touch of well-integrated oak in youth (30 to 40 percent new barrels are used for aging), freshness, and minerality. It is a classic Graves that displays a certain elegance and smoky, tobacco aromas with age. Both the red and the white are a rather good value.

In 1989 the *cuverie* was renovated, and the old wooden vats were replaced by temperature-controlled stainless steel tanks. Around the same time a second wine, Lagrave Martillac, was introduced to improve selection; the *grand vin* today represents approximately 70 percent of the production. The main changes since then have been work in the vineyards and the reduction in yields. As Tristan Kressmann points out, the average yield for both red and white wines over the last 10 years has been 40 to 45 hectoliters per hectare, whereas in 1990 it was closer to 60.

and Loïc, took over running the estate and continue today (the property is now owned by Jean's many children), while a new perspective was given to the wine-making with the recruitment of oenologist Valérie Vialard, vineyard manager Denis Wendling, and advice from consultant oenologists Professor Denis Dubourdieu and Michel Rolland.

Régis Marcon

Loire Zander Meunière with Harmony of Jerusalem Artichoke and Almond

For the Almond Milk. Infuse the almonds in warm milk for 1 hour. Strain and chill until needed.

For the Jerusalem Artichoke Purée. Peel half of the tubers and cut into large cubes. Cook in the vegetable stock for 20 to 30 minutes. Purée the artichokes in a blender, gradually adding the warm milk and cream. Keep the purée warm.

Peel the remaining artichokes and dice small. Heat up a sauté pan and brown the artichoke dice. Keep the dice warm.

For the Mushroom Sauce. Brown the mushrooms in the pan, then deglaze with the soy sauce, lemon juice, and balsamic vinegar. Pour in enough water to cover the mushrooms and cook for 10 minutes. Strain and then reduce the sauce. Set aside. Melt the butter just until it turns a nutty brown. Strain and keep chilled.

For the Zander. In a pan, sauté the zander fillets, skin side down, in hot butter with the crushed garlic clove and thyme. Baste frequently with the melted butter.

When the fish is cooked, add the artichoke dice to each serving plate and top with a zander fillet. Pour the artichoke purée around the fish. Add a small amount of the browned butter to the mushroom sauce. Pour the sauce on each plate. Beat the almond milk to a froth and serve separately.

Ingredients
Serves 4

For the Almond Milk
- 1 cup (250 ml) milk
- ⅓ cup (50 g) sweet almonds
- ⅓ cup (50 g) bitter almonds

For the Jerusalem Artichoke Purée
- 1 pound (500 g) Jerusalem artichokes
- Vegetable stock
- 1 tablespoon whole milk
- 1 tablespoon heavy cream
- 1 tablespoon olive oil

For the Mushroom Sauce
- 2 ½ cups (200 g) button mushrooms, quartered
- 3 ½ tablespoons (50 ml) soy sauce
- Juice of 1 lemon
- 3 ½ tablespoons (50 ml) balsamic vinegar
- 2 tablespoons (30 g) unsalted butter

For the Zander
- 4 river zander fillets
- 3 ½ tablespoons (50 g) unsalted butter
- 1 garlic clove, crushed
- 1 sprig thyme

Château Latour-Martillac blanc 1998

A full and generous white wine with touches of hazelnut and almond that blend in with the sauce and accompaniment. The hint of bitterness balances with the Jerusalem artichoke. A wine as fine and distinct as ever, it is the perfect complement to the exquisite texture of the zander.

—Laurent Blanchon, Sommelier

Château
Laville Haut-Brion

One of the most singular and long-lived dry white wines in the world, Château Laville Haut-Brion holds its place in the pantheon of dry white stars. Comparisons with fine white Burgundy are not inappropriate, as the Sémillon-based wine is pure, clean, and crystalline in youth but gains honeyed complexity with age.

The best place to view the vineyard of Château Laville Haut-Brion is from the university campus in the Bordeaux suburb of Talence. Students in the residence above have a bird's-eye view of the three tiny parcels of Sémillon and Sauvignon Blanc that produce the wine. The oldest was planted in 1934, the others in 1960 and 1961. Surrounding these is the "mother" vineyard of Château La Mission Haut-Brion.

One of the most singular and long-lived dry white wines in the world, Château Laville Haut-Brion is part of the stable of properties, including Châteaux Haut-Brion and La Mission Haut-Brion, owned by the American Dillon family. It is actually produced at La Mission but was

classified independently in 1953 and has such a unique character that it merits its own distinctive status.

The birth of this wine came about through the fusion of two separate vineyards, Clos Laville and La Mission Haut-Brion *Blanc*. The Laville estate has a well-documented history. Originally known as Terrefort, it was acquired by Marie Laville in 1611 and stayed in the family until 1717 when it was bought by a Bordeaux surgeon, Bernard Gaussens, who changed the name to Laville.

From 1782 until 1912 there followed a sequence of owners, principally the Bouscasse

Château Laville Haut-Brion

family, who were involved in the Bordeaux wine trade either as *négociants* or *courtiers*. The wine produced was red, and it was not until after 1912, when the property was acquired by a local barrel merchant named Léopold Bibonne, that the first white grape varieties are believed to have been planted. In 1931 Clos Laville again changed hands, this time purchased by Frédéric Woltner, the owner of neighboring Château La Mission Haut-Brion. Historical records now owned by the Dillon family show an absence of white grape varieties at La Mission when Woltner acquired the estate in 1919. However, they were evidently planted in the interim, as in 1927 through 1930 four vintages of Château La Mission Haut-Brion *Blanc* were produced.

The purchase of Clos Laville brought the Woltners a further 2.5 hectares of vineyard producing a small volume of red (labelled Clos du Domaine Saint-Sauveur) and 33.75 hectoliters (in 1928) of white wine. The latter was immediately integrated into La Mission *Blanc*, resulting in the first vintage of Château Laville—Terroir du Haut-Brion in 1931—renamed Château Laville Haut-Brion for the 1934 vintage. In 1983 the Dillon family acquired both Laville and La Mission Haut-Brion.

The intrinsic character of Laville Haut-Brion is closely related to the unusual dominance of Sémillon in the blend. A good 80 percent is the norm (86 percent, for instance, in 2006), with a complement of Sauvignon Blanc. The vines are low yielding and the wine rich, opulent, and intense in youth with balancing acidity, a marked note of citrus fruit, and a touch of vanilla oak. Greater purity of fruit has been the

defining factor in recent years, giving the wine further precision and length.

An important part of the Laville legend is the wine's ability to age. Accessible in the first two to three years, it then closes up before reopening at eight to ten years with a more complex form and expression. Thirty to forty years is the potential for some vintages, the Sémillon maintaining freshness but providing a creamy texture on the palate and a panoply of aromas that vary from biscuity to waxy, honeyed notes and even crystallized fruits. A fine white Burgundy would be the nearest comparison to make with Laville.

Proximity to the university means no lack of pickers come harvest time. The grapes are selectively harvested by *tris* or successive passages

through the vines, then pressed and the juice cold settled. The fermentation is started in stainless steel vats and completed in oak barrels, 50 percent of which are new. There is no malolactic fermentation, but the wine is matured on stirred lees in barrel for ten months prior to bottling.

In the past the percentage of Sauvignon Blanc was a little higher in Laville Haut-Brion, as was the volume of wine, but in 1990 a part of the vineyard was replanted to Merlot and Cabernet Sauvignon for La Mission Haut-Brion. By the late 2000s the vineyard comprised just 2.55 hectares, producing between 7,200 and 9,600 exceptional bottles a year.

Alain Passard
Celeriac Stack with Chestnuts and Black Périgord Truffle

Ingredients
Serves 4
- 1 celeriac, preferably Monarch
- Whole milk
- Salted butter
- 1 packet vacuum-packed chestnuts
- Homemade breadcrumbs
- 1 black Périgord truffle (*tuber melanosporum*)
- Flat-leaf parsley
- Fleur de sel (coarse sea salt from Guérande)
- Ground allspice

For the Celeriac. Wash the celeriac without removing its leafy part. Cut the vegetable vertically into slices ¼ inch (½ cm) thick.

Lay the celeriac flat in a large pan, pour in just enough milk to cover the slices, add a knob of salted butter, and cook for 10 to 12 minutes. Cover with parchment paper to contain the aromas, flavors, and colors in the pan. When done, leave the celeriac slices to cool down in their cooking juices.

Drain the slices and lay them flat on a baking tray. Sprinkle flakes of chestnut over each slice; then, using a pastry brush, dab the chestnut flakes with melted butter. Sprinkle a thin layer of breadcrumbs over the celeriac, sparingly; you should still be able to see the chestnut flakes through the veil of breadcrumbs.

Place the celeriac slices under a grill to brown the breadcrumbs, 7 to 8 minutes depending on your grill. Leave a gap of around 4 inches (10 cm) between the grill and the vegetable to obtain a lovely golden crust.

Stack the celeriac slices on a serving dish, letting each slice slightly overlap. Sprinkle with the truffle, finely sliced using a mandoline, the freshly chopped parsley, coarse sea salt, and allspice.

Château Laville Haut-Brion 2006

The gradation of color is wonderfully highlighted with silver reflections. Citrus and mineral notes reach the nose first, followed by white flowers and acacia, to create an intense, complex, and delectable bouquet. The palate is tight and precise. Wonderful richness provides the perfect balance. Flavors of citrus add a pleasant zing that develops into a spicy finish, including a note of saffron. This wine enhances the flavors of the celeriac stack. Vivacious and intense, it is the perfect foil for this very aromatic dish and has the breadth and depth to support the truffle.

—Guillaume Muller, Sommelier

Château
Malartic-Lagravière

A "sleeping beauty" awakened from its slumbers in 1997, Malartic-Lagravière has been transformed in little more than a decade. A new château and cellars have risen while the vineyard has steadily expanded. There's a distinct new swagger to the wines, the red now bright and vigorous, the white ripe and round.

Above:
Hand-harvesting
in *cagettes* (crates).

Opposite:
Sorting berries and filling
vats by gravity.

Château Malartic-Lagravière was a "sleeping beauty" when Belgian businessman Alfred-Alexandre Bonnie bestowed the awakening kiss in 1997. Seemingly overnight the gravelly vineyard was revitalized and a new state-of-the-art winery was in place. The wines, too, took on a new expression, the reds with added vigor, length, and finesse, the whites with fuller, riper fruit.

Domaine de Lagravière, as it was once known, owes its name to the deep gravel terrace (26 feet [8 meters] deep in places) that constitutes the heart of the vineyard. In 1803 it was purchased by Pierre de Malartic, nephew of Comte Hippolyte de Maurès de Malartic, an admiral of the fleet who fought the English in Quebec and later became governor of Mauritius.

A replica of his ship, *La Minerve*, now greets visitors to Château Malartic-Lagravière, and the image has been used on the labels since the 1996 vintage. The change of name, though, occurred in 1850, when the property was bought by Madame Arnaud Ricard, who, in deference to the admiral, added the Malartic name.

The estate eventually passed to her granddaughter, Angèle, who in 1876 married a certain Lucien Ridoret. Her father-in-law, Laurent, was also a seagoing man (mercantile rather than navy), and it was the image of his three-mast ship, the *Marie-Elisabeth*, that was initially used on the Malartic labels beginning in 1983.

The property remained in family hands, becoming one of the leading wines of the Graves area, with the red being classified in 1953 and the white in 1959. But there followed an inauspicious period from the 1960s into the 1980s when the red was lean and tough and only the white wine retained some renown.

In 1990 Malartic was sold to the champagne house Laurent-Perrier. The 19-hectare vineyard was well maintained, but otherwise little investment was made and the wines remained on the whole unexceptional. In the meantime, Laurent-Perrier needed some financing, so the property was again put up for sale and in 1997 was purchased by Alfred-Alexandre Bonnie, who had been searching for a pedigreed Bordeaux estate for a number of years.

An impressive budget of several million euros was earmarked for the revival of Malartic-Lagravière. Because the buildings and cellars in use were those constructed by the Ricard family in the 19th century, the Bonnies decided to rebuild both the château and the technical facilities. The new winery, which is gravity-fed and contains both stainless steel and wooden vats for vinification and cellars with a capacity of 1,200 barrels of red wine and 200 of white,

was completed for the 1998 vintage. It is from this point that a distinct improvement in quality can be noted.

The personnel also needed to be reconsidered, as previously Malartic-Lagravière had been managed from a distance by Laurent-Perrier. A young *maître de chais* was engaged, a trained vineyard manager, and Michel Rolland retained as consultant oenologist. In 2003 Alfred-Alexandre Bonnie placed the overall management in the hands of his son Jean-Jacques and his daughter-in-law Séverine.

The vineyard also experienced a major overhaul. Of the original 19 hectares, two were grubbed up, and extra parcels were planted. Eleven hectares of a neighboring vineyard known as Château Neuf were purchased and planted, as well as a 7-hectare parcel called Marquet that had once been part of the

Domaine de Lagravière. On the other side of the town of Léognan, at a site known as Laguloup, further planting on land that had not been cultivated since the 1950s was done. All told the vineyard now totals 53 hectares, 7 of which are white.

Previously the Malartic white was traditionally made of pure Sauvignon Blanc and rather crisp and citric. The Bonnies, though, planted Sémillon and it now represents up to 20 percent in the blend. Riper fruit and the addition of Sémillon have introduced an exotic note and given the wine a broader, fuller feel.

The red is made from a varying blend of 45 percent Cabernet Sauvignon, 45 percent Merlot, 8 percent Cabernet Franc, and 2 percent Petit Verdot aged for 15 to 22 months in 50 to 70 percent new oak barrels. With the considerable number of new plantings, the *grand vin* in the

2000s represented only 45 percent of the production, the rest going into the second wine, La Réserve de Malartic, also called Le Sillage de Malartic (a nautical reference again, *sillage* meaning the wake of the label's boat). In time the *grand vin* is expected to rise gradually to 60 percent of the production.

The rate of change at Château Malartic-Lagravière has been vertiginous to say the least. The Bonnies, though, look at it as a long-term project, which bodes well for the future of the estate.

Above:
The red barrel cellar.
Opposite:
A winter scene at Malartic.

Éric Ripert
Thinly Pounded Yellowfin Tuna, Foie Gras, and Toasted Baguette

For the Foie Gras Terrine. Place the lobe in ice water and refrigerate overnight. Remove the foie gras from the water and pat dry. Cover with plastic wrap and let stand at room temperature for 1 hour. Separate the two lobes, keeping one covered while you work on the other. Starting at the primary vein on the underside of the foie gras, carefully slice through the lobe to the main vein. Split the foie gras apart and butterfly the lobe by making an outward cut at each side of the vein. Remove the primary vein and then the small veins throughout the foie gras. Repeat with the remaining lobe. Mix the salt, pepper, and sel rose together. Season the foie gras evenly on both sides. Cover with plastic wrap and refrigerate for 24 hours. Form the foie gras into a log, approximately 2 ½ inches (6 cm) wide by 6 inches (15 cm) long, on a piece of parchment paper, twisting and squeezing the ends so it is compact. Unwrap the foie gras and transfer it to a piece of cheesecloth. Rolling away from you, roll the foie gras into a tight log, again twisting the ends to compact the shape. Tie one end of the cheesecloth with a piece of kitchen twine and then the other end. Meanwhile, bring the chicken stock to a boil in a pot large enough to hold the foie gras. Add the foie gras to the stock and cook for 2 minutes, or until it reaches an internal temperature of 90°F (32°C). Remove from the stock and chill immediately. Refrigerate overnight. Remove the cheesecloth and reshape the torchon one more time with plastic wrap. Refrigerate overnight.

For the Tuna. Slice the tuna into ¼-inch-thick slices. Lay a large sheet of plastic wrap on a work surface, at least 2 x 3 feet (60 x 90 cm). Arrange the tuna pieces, with 1 inch (2.5 cm) between each slice, on the plastic; cover the tuna with another large sheet of plastic. Using a kitchen mallet, gently pound the tuna until there is a very thin and even layer about ⅛ inch (3 mm) thick. Using the template and a sharp knife, cut through the tuna and both layers of plastic to get four marquise-shaped portions. Refrigerate the tuna for at least 30 minutes; it can be pounded and cut a few hours ahead of time.

Preheat the oven to 350°F (175°C). Slice the bread lengthwise into 4 very thin slices. Arrange the slices on a parchment paper-lined baking sheet; cover with parchment paper and another baking sheet (so the slices stay as flat as possible). Toast the slices in a 350°F (175°C) oven until they are lightly browned and crisp, 5 to 7 minutes. Allow the slices to cool to room temperature.

Slice four thin pieces, approximately ⅛ inch (3 mm) thick, of foie gras, making sure each slice is as long as the baguette slices. Place the foie gras slices on top of the baguette slices. Place each baguette in the center of an oval-shaped plate. Pull the top piece of plastic wrap off of a portion of tuna. Invert the tuna (so the remaining plastic-wrapped side is in your hand) and place it on top of the foie gras baguette. Pull the other piece of plastic wrap off. Season the tuna, and brush with extra-virgin olive oil. Sprinkle shallots and chives over each of the fillets. Squeeze lemon juice over each portion and serve immediately.

Ingredients
Serves 4

For the Foie Gras Terrine
- 1 lobe foie gras, approximately 1 ½ pounds (700g)
- 1 tablespoon (10 g) fine sea salt
- 2 pinches (½ teaspoon) freshly ground white pepper
- A pinch (¼ teaspoon) sel rose
- 6 cups (150 cl) chicken stock

For the Tuna
- 12 ounces (350 g) sushi-quality yellowfin tuna fillet
- Marquise-shaped 4 ½ x 9-inch (11.5 x 23 cm) template

For the Garnish
- 1 mini baguette
- Fine sea salt and freshly ground white pepper
- 4 tablespoons (60 ml) extra-virgin olive oil
- 2 teaspoons (10 g) shallots, peeled and minced
- 2 tablespoons (6 g) thinly sliced chives
- 1 lemon, cut in half

Château Malartic-Lagravière blanc 2002

At once crisp and fresh, this white Malartic 2002 develops an elegant full body on the palate, balanced out by a lively acidity that picks up the flavors of the olive oil and tuna. The beautiful aromatic structure of the wine, intense and complex, delivers a superb finish, while the blend of clean fruit and elegant mineral notes combines wonderfully with the foie gras and baguette.

—**Aldo Sohm**, Sommelier

Château Olivier

A historic estate with a moated château 7 miles (11 kilometers) from the center of Bordeaux, Olivier continues to evolve as a viticultural domaine. A new vineyard site in the forested parkland, old parcels restructured, renovated cellars: the early 2000s have been anything but inactive years.

It's a secret world hidden from view a mere 7 miles (11 kilometers) from the center of Bordeaux. Centennial oaks and clusters of pine form a forested driveway leading to a paradise of meadow, park, vineyards, and moated château, the origins of which date from the 12th century. This is Château Olivier, a family-owned property and one of the most splendid of Bordeaux.

The forest is deep and dense, and accounts for two-thirds of the 220-hectare estate, much of it included in the appellation zone. The Black Prince, it is claimed, hunted these woods in the late 14th century and used the original château, "La Salle de Léognan" as it was known, as a hunting lodge. By this time the *seigneurie* of

Olivier had already been in existence for some 200 years.

Down through the centuries Olivier remained a "noble" estate; it was owned in the 17th century by the Baron de La Brède and later the Baron de Montesquieu (father of the celebrated writer and philosopher). In the 18th century the château was extensively renovated, providing much of the style seen today. It was later, in 1963, declared a historic monument.

The Bethmann family, originally a banking dynasty from Frankfurt, acquired the property in 1886 and it has remained in the same family ever since. Jean-Jacques de Bethmann, the latest

incumbent and resident landlord, has been running the estate since 1981. His driving ambition, now fulfilled, was to secure the succession for the next generation.

Changes first began to occur in the early 1980s under the direction of Jean-Jacques de Bethmann. New oak barrels were brought in for aging and for the fermentation of the white wine, until then vinified and aged in vat, and in the vineyards there was an increase in the planting of Merlot. This was nothing, though, compared to the revolution that has taken place since 2002.

Under the leadership of a young managing director, Laurent Lebrun, a detailed inventory of the soils was undertaken that included as many as 200 analyses. In an inspired move, the analysis was also conducted on a forested area to

the west of the property, where a mound of gravel compacted with sand and clay was found, ideal for cultivating the vine.

Confirmation of the site's potential was validated by a glance at the famous 18th-century map compiled by the engineer Belleyme, which shows vines planted at this location, known locally as Bel-Air. Since 2004, 6.5 hectares of Cabernet Sauvignon have been planted on the 8-hectare site, which has an elevation of 180 feet (55 meters).

The study identified 11 different types of soil at Château Olivier, causing the owners to reflect on the structure of the vineyard and usher in a more thorough plot-by-plot management scheme. Parcels of vines on the original vineyard, a mound to the east of the château, have been

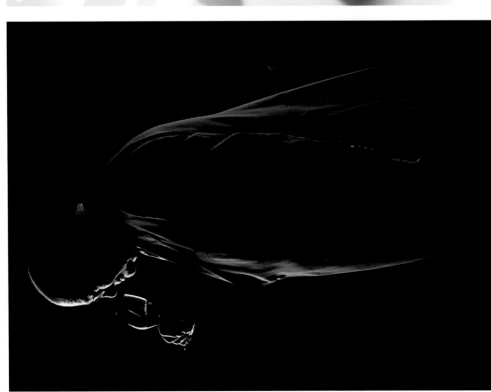

range of smaller stainless steel tanks that would help take the concept of plot-by-plot management to its full conclusion in the winery. A barrel cellar completed in 1997 houses the barrels for maturing the red wine, one third of which are renewed each year.

The white wines are now lively, fresh, and aromatic, the reds medium-bodied, ripe, and elegant, with greater precision of fruit. And with the new vineyards coming into production, one can only speculate on advances to come. The Bethmanns now have a quality of wine to match their magical realm.

dug up and replanted on more appropriate soil. Sémillon and Sauvignon Blanc, for instance, have been relocated to limestone-based soil, while Merlot has been planted on clay-gravel soil in a formerly forested area.

Still "a work in progress," the vineyard today represents 60 hectares planted, 15 percent with white varieties. Château Olivier *blanc* is traditionally a 50/50 blend of Sémillon and Sauvignon Blanc, but vintages in the later part of this decade are likely to have a greater percentage of Sauvignon Blanc. The red wine is produced from a blend of 50 percent Cabernet Sauvignon, 45 percent Merlot, and 5 percent Cabernet Franc.

The change of politics in the vineyard necessitated changes in the cellars as well. In 2003 a new *cuverie* constructed within the original 18th-century building was revealed complete with a

Jacques and Laurent Pourcel

Roasted Pigeon Fillets, Curried Giblet Pastillas, and Pan-fried Pears

To prepare the Pigeons. Flambé and then trim the pigeons: Cut away the thighs, remove the wings, carve the fillets, keep the livers and hearts. Set the fillets aside and bone the thighs.

For the Pastillas. In a sauté pan, fry the wings with half of the thighs. Add the chopped shallots and deglaze the pan with the white wine. Let reduce and add water to moisten. Add salt and the curry and cinnamon powders. Cook until the meat is tender enough to break away easily. Reduce completely. Remove any bones that have come away. Allow to cool and then mix and mash the ingredients together with a fork. Fold in the egg and then the cream. Season to taste with salt and pepper.

Cut the phyllo pastry sheets into 6 triangles. Put 1 tablespoon of pigeon meat and a few caramelized almonds on each triangle. Roll into a ball, sprinkle lightly with curry powder and cover with another pastry triangle. Brush with clarified butter and sprinkle with confectioners' sugar.

For the Sauce. Sweat the chopped shallots in 1 knob of butter, moisten with red wine and reduce until dry. Set aside. Put 2 tablespoons (30 g) of butter and the cocoa powder in a hot sauté pan. Cook over low heat. Add the ganache, half of the pigeon livers, the sugar, the shallots preserved in wine, the blanched garlic, the pigeon jus, and the balsamic vinegar. Season. Reduce by half and then thicken with 1 ½ tablespoons (20 g) of butter. Blend. Put the mixture through a sieve and season to taste. Peel and core the pears. Quarter the pears and sauté them in a nonstick pan with a knob of butter.

To cook the Pigeons. Chop the remaining thighs, bacon, livers, and hearts into large cubes. Thread each type of meat in turn onto skewers (allowing one per person). Pan-fry the kebabs in butter and season to taste.

Flash-roast the pigeon fillets and feet for around 5 minutes in a casserole with 1 tablespoon of peanut oil. Bake the pastillas in the oven at 350°F (180°C) until they turn lightly golden.

Heat up the celery purée. Cut each pigeon fillet in half. Add 1 tablespoon of celery purée in the center of the plate and top with the pastilla. Surround with the pigeon fillets, the kebabs, and the pear quarters. Dress with the sauce. Garnish with herbs, cocoa, and curry powder. Serve immediately.

Ingredients
Serves 4

- 4 pigeons

For the Pastillas
- 1 shallot
- 1 scant cup (200 ml) white wine
- Curry powder
- 1 pinch cinnamon powder
- 1 egg
- ¼ cup heavy cream (50 ml)
- 3 phyllo pastry sheets
- ½ cup (40 g) flaked almonds, caramelized in sugar
- ¼ cup (60 g) clarified butter
- 1 teaspoon confectioners' sugar
- Salt and white pepper

For the Sauce
- 1 shallot, chopped
- 5 tablespoons (80 g) unsalted butter
- 1 scant cup (200 ml) red wine
- 2 tablespoons bitter cocoa powder
- 1 tablespoon dark ganache (equal measures of chocolate and heavy cream)
- 3 pigeon livers
- 2 teaspoons superfine sugar
- 1 tablespoon chopped shallots preserved in wine
- 3 garlic cloves, blanched 4 times
- 1 cup (250 ml) pigeon jus (or veal jus will also do)
- 1 tablespoon balsamic vinegar
- 2 pears
- 1 ¾ ounces (50 g) barding or bacon fat
- 1 knob butter
- ½ cup (100 g) celery purée
- 1 tablespoon peanut oil

Château Olivier rouge 2001

We chose this dish to match a 2001 vintage Château Olivier, powerful in its elegance. The pigeon, accompanied by the giblet pastilla, will balance the bottle's Cabernet, whose aromatic notes of slightly jammy red fruits and spices will make an interesting marriage with the pink flesh and pronounced taste of the giblets.

The Merlot lends a hint of mineral and softens the tannins. The velvety, soft, and concentrated palate conjures up the sweetness of pear, while the toasty finish pleasantly complements the bitter cocoa jus.

To sum up, we are pairing a plump, concentrated yet wonderfully fine wine with a dish complex in both flavor and texture.

—Yannis Kherachi, Sommelier

Château
Pape Clément

Seven hundred years of history are embodied in this wine, from the medieval patronage of Pope Clément V to the present-day direction of owner Bernard Magrez. Assertive but seductive in style, ripe and modern in its youth but gaining smoky Graves complexity with age, Pape Clément continues to endure the test of time.

Seven hundred years of history are embodied in this wine, from the medieval patronage of its most celebrated owner, Pope Clément V, to the present-day command of proprietor Bernard Magrez. Urbanization, oidium, phylloxera, and even a devastating hailstorm in 1937 could have spelled the end of this property, but it survived, establishing its position as a leading *cru* in the Graves and even Bordeaux.

The end seemed near when, in 1938, Pape Clément was sold to real estate developers, but luckily the project never came to fruition. Now the 32-hectare vineyard with a park and 19th-century château stands as an oasis within Pessac's suburban sprawl. Traffic on Bordeaux's busy beltway, the *rocade*, flows close by while aircraft overhead highlight the proximity of Mérignac airport.

The site is part of what used to be an extensive area of viticultural land, the core of the old vineyards of the Graves. The soils are essentially Pyrenean gravel with varying percentages of sand, clay, and pebbles, depending on the parcel. Cabernet Sauvignon has been planted to 60 percent, with Merlot the accompanying variety (although traditionally the wine is often a 50/50 blend of the two).

Dark in color, the *cru classé* red of Pape Clément is both assertive and seductive. Rich, ripe, and slightly oaky when young, it gains in aromatic complexity, with smoky, spicy notes becoming more apparent with age. The palate is firm and forceful, the sweetness of fruit underpinned by a strong tannic frame and a minerality that provides balancing freshness and length.

Opposite, bottom left: Bernard Magrez.

The insignia of a papal tiara and crossed keys embossed on the bottle and inscribed on the label is a constant reminder of the origins of the domaine. On his appointment as Archbishop of Bordeaux in 1299, Bertrand de Goth received as a gift from his brother, Gaillard, a small estate in Pessac known as the Domaine de la Mothe (*mothe* being a medieval term for raised land). The property consisted of a residence, wood, and two parcels of vines. Six years later Bertrand was elected pope, taking the name Clément V. Prior to his departure to the papal seat in Avignon in 1309, the new pope donated La Mothe to the archbishopric of Bordeaux. The vineyard gradually took the name of Pape Clément (the first specific mention appears in 1561). The property remained in the hands of the church until the Revolution.

After the Revolution the banker Charles Peixotto became the first lay owner of the Pape Clément vines, purchasing the 4-hectare vineyard in 1791. It was enlarged, then sold in 1810 to the mayor of Pessac, Firmin Jarrige, who amalgamated it with a neighboring property known as the Domaine de Sainte-Marie de Belair, which he had acquired in 1805.

This expanded estate was again sold, in 1858, to the *négociant* Jean-Baptiste Clerc. He restored and expanded the vineyard, particularly after the ravages of oidium and phylloxera, and instituted the name of Château Pape Clément. He also constructed the present château, which was extensively remodeled by his successors, whose additions included medieval ramparts and tower and gothic elements.

Château Pape Clément

Another change of ownership occurred in 1890. Following the near disastrous hailstorm and buyout by developers in 1937–38, Pape Clément was acquired by Paul Montagne in 1939. Throughout this period of change in the late 19th and early 20th centuries the wines of Pape Clément remained highly regarded, as they did into the 1950s and 1960s. A leaner period, however, ensued in the 1970s and early 1980s.

The modern renaissance of Château Pape Clément dates from 1985 and coincides with a change of management and the arrival of Bernard Magrez at the helm. New wine-making facilities were built, the barrel cellar restored, and in 1986 a second wine, Le Clémentin, introduced to improve selection. Of more long-term importance, a program for replanting and restructuring the vineyard was initiated, which has since led to the renewal of 60 percent of its surface area.

There has been further change and innovation in the 21st century. During the harvest an army of nearly 150 people sort and de-stem the grapes by hand. These are picked parcel by parcel, and the separation continues through to vinification in a bank of brand new wooden vats. The use of pumps is avoided; the grapes and later the wine are gravity fed. Pape Clément also produces a tiny quantity of fine but rare white wine from Sémillon, Sauvignon Blanc, and Muscadelle.

Such a long and illustrious history enhances the appreciation of the wine. Pope Clément V may remain innocent of his creation, but he launched a label and a wine that have endured the test of time.

Michel Guérard

Noix of Veal Cheek "Chabrol" with Grilled Prawns

Ingredients
Serves 6

For the Braising Stock
- 1 bottle (750 ml) red wine
- 3 ⅛ cups (750 ml) veal stock

For the Veal Cheeks
- 6 veal cheeks, 4 ¼ to 5 ounces (120 to 140 g) each
- Olive oil
- 4 tablespoons (60 g) butter
- ¾ cup (100 g) carrot, cut into mirepoix
- ¾ cup (100 g) onion, cut into mirepoix
- 2 garlic cloves
- ¼ cup (40 g) shallots
- 1 preserved lemon, cut into 8
- Zest of 1 lemon
- 1 sugar cube

For the Bouquet Garni
- 1 ½ ounces (40 g) leek greens (about two leek leaves)
- 5 sprigs thyme
- 1 bay leaf
- 4 sprigs coriander
- 4 sprigs parsley
- 1 sprig mint

For the Candied Carrots
- 1 pound (500 g) carrots
- Juice of 1 orange
- 1 tablespoon (20 g) honey
- 2 tablespoons (30 ml) olive oil

For the Herb Salad
- ½ bunch chervil (leaves only)
- ½ bunch chives
- ¼ bunch flat-leaf parsley
- ¼ bunch coriander
- 1 Granny Smith apple
- 1 lemon
- 6 Madagascar prawns (40/60 count)

For the Braising Stock. Boil and flambé the wine. Add the veal stock. Set aside.

For the Veal Cheeks. Trim the veal cheeks and remove the nerves from each side of the cheeks. Season and brown the cheeks in a pan with the olive oil. Once the cheeks are nicely browned, add the other ingredients: the carrots, onion, garlic, shallots, preserved lemon, lemon zest, and sugar cube. Lightly brown the mixture, removing any excess fat as necessary. Pour the contents of the pan into a cooking pot suitable for the oven. Add the braising stock and bouquet garni. Skim off any scum and cook for 2 ½ hours at 275°F (160°C). The meat should be soft and tender.

Remove the veal cheeks from the pot and place on a perforated baking tray. Cover with plastic wrap so they do not dry out. Pour the braising stock through a strainer and reduce by three-quarters until it thickens. Emulsify the reduced stock with the butter. Reheat the cheeks in the sauce just before serving.

For the Candied Carrots. Peel the carrots and cut them into diagonal slices about ⅛ inch (3 mm) thick using a mandoline. Cook in boiling salted water. Drain and place the carrot slices in a saucepan with the juice of the orange, the honey, and the olive oil. Bring to a boil and cook until the carrots are nicely glazed.

For the Herb Salad. Remove the leaves from the stems and mix together. About 30 minutes before serving, cut the apple into matchsticks (julienne) and place them in cold water with a dash of lemon juice to prevent them from browning. Grill the prawns, *a la plancha*, and thread them onto a bamboo skewer. Keep warm in a 300°F (150°C) oven. Meanwhile, reheat the carrots and place them on a warm dinner plate.

Arrange the carrots elegantly on each serving plate. Gently lay each veal cheek on top of the carrots, the herb salad to one side of the cheek, the julienne of apple on the herb salad, and the prawn skewer on the other side of the cheek. Serve immediately.

Château Pape Clément rouge 2005

The noix of veal cheek "chabrol" with grilled prawns is a smooth and tender dish, designed for maximum aroma, which offers a near perfect pairing with the Pape Clément. This wine provides just the right sense of balance and harmony, especially from such a great vintage year as 2005: the powerful, velvety wine marries well with the generosity of this rustic yet elegant dish.

—Oriane Chambon and Stéphane Obeltz, Sommeliers

Château
Smith Haut Lafitte

Since Daniel and Florence Cathiard acquired the estate in 1990, the property has been transformed beyond recognition, as has the quality of its wines. The change is evident not only in the *cuverie* and the hotel-spa complex, Les Sources de Caudalie, but also in the wines, which are now ripe and generous.

Opposite:
Surrounded by woodland at the gateway to Bordeaux, the Château's vines roll across the hill ("Lafitte" or "Lafite" in old French), while Les Sources de Caudalie welcomes epicureans.

Above:
The yellow roses are a nod to the fleur-de-lis on the coat of arms; the bronze hare reflects the vine-growing artisanship that is ever-present on the Château grounds.

A number of the *Crus Classés* of Graves have benefited from the energy and commitment of new ownership in recent years, and none more so than Château Smith Haut Lafitte. Since the Cathiards, Daniel and Florence, purchased the estate in 1990, both the property and the wines have been completely overhauled.

The visible signs of this renaissance are abundant: the renovated 18th-century *chartreuse*, which is now the Cathiards' home; the remodeled 16th-century tower; the new *cuverie* and barrel cellar for white wine; additional tasting and function rooms; and the artwork (notably the Barry Flanagan sculpture of a flying hare), not to mention the adjacent hotel-spa complex, Les Sources de Caudalie. The fundamentals, too, have not been forgotten: the vineyard has been restructured and restored.

So much has happened since 1990 that it's easy to forget Smith Haut Lafitte's long history, which can be traced back to the 14th century. At this time the vine was cultivated here by the *maison noble* du Boscq. Later, in the 17th century, the Verrier family, now owners of du Boscq, continued the construction of the vineyard on the plateau known locally as Lafitte, distinguished by its Gunzian gravel soil.

In 1720 the property was bought by George Smith, a British *négociant* who gave the estate its present name. Through marriage and inheritance it eventually came under the ownership of Lodi-Martin Duffour-Dubergier, mayor of Bordeaux, in 1842. The estate expanded further, and by the turn of the century it numbered 270 hectares, of which 68 were planted with red varieties. There was also a vineyard of white

Château Smith Haut Lafitte

Above:
For thousands of years,
the Garonne has brought
Gunzian gravel in between
the rows of vines at Smith
Haut Lafitte. These shiny
pebbles help the grape
berries to ripen before they
are sorted almost
individually and delicately
transported in small oak
barrels.

Following pages, left:
Over 1,000 Château Smith
Haut Lafitte and Les Hauts
de Smith barrels are
matured together beneath
the ancient vaults of the
cavernous underground
barrel cellar.

Right, top left:
In summer and winter,
the *Vénus Bordeaux* by
sculptor Jim Dine keeps
watch over the old Cabernet
Sauvignons.

Right, bottom left:
The château's cooper fits a
chestnut hoop around a
barrel, which he makes
every day with select oak
from Tronçay Forest.

banned from 1992 on. Plowing has been used since 1991 on the whole estate, and since 2000 the parcels of Sauvignon Blanc have been worked with horses. From 1995 on they have used mating disruption instead of insecticides in the fight against the grape berry moth, and their own organic compost from 1997 on.

With the idea of sustainable viticulture in mind, the Cathiards set about restricting the yields and restructuring the vineyard. Two important decisions were made. Five hectares of vineyard on the present site of the hotel-spa were uprooted and the Cabernet Sauvignon replanted on better, more gravelly soil across the road; and in the northern part of the estate Cabernet Sauvignon that had difficulty ripening on clay soils was replaced with Merlot. All told, 30 percent of the vineyard has been reconstituted, with a current surface area of 67 hectares.

varieties producing a yearly volume of 12 tonneaux (14,400 bottles) of wine.

The *négociant* house of Louis Eschenauer took an interest in the estate in 1902, initially leasing the property and eventually buying it in 1958. Although the red wine was classified in 1953, there was no classification for whites during this period. Eschenauer, as owner, planted Sauvignon Blanc and made other investments in the vineyard and winery, including the construction of a vaulted underground cellar that can hold 2,000 barrels. The wine, though, remained uneven until the 1980s, when it started to improve.

When the Cathiards purchased the property in 1990, they quickly realized that the mechanical cultivation practiced by Eschenauer had to be reversed. Hand picking was reintroduced for the first harvest in 1991 and weed killers were

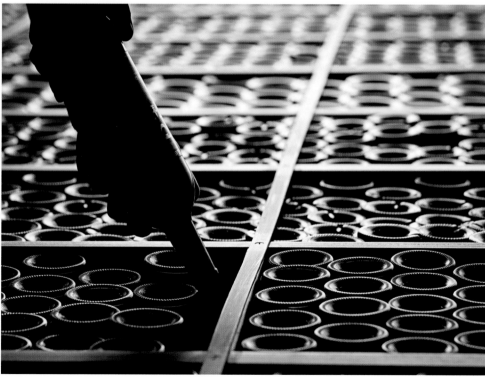

Above:
Since 1991, Daniel and Florence Cathiard have dedicated their lives to seeing that the character of their historic terroir is fully expressed in the glass.

Opposite:
They enjoy welcoming tasters to the newly rebuilt George Smith Orangery with its unique underground "paradise".

The vineyard has been the main focus of improvements at Smith Haut Lafitte, but there's been plenty of action at the winery as well. A cooperage integrated into the château in 1995 supplies 60 percent of the estate's needs (the red is aged in 60 to 80 percent new oak barrels, depending on the vintage), and since 2000 only truncated wooden vats have been used for fermenting the reds. A barrel cellar for the white wine was created in 1995 and improvements made to the vaulted red cellar, including a "double lining" around the walls for perfect temperature control.

With the help of consultants and skilled young winemakers, the wines have become stronger and stronger. The barrel-fermented white was the first to garner approval since the 1993 vintage. Sauvignon Gris was planted to supplement the Sauvignon Blanc, improving the wine's aromatic complexity, and since 2002 a little Sémillon has been added as well. The style is full and ripe, elegant and fresh on the finish.

The red took a little longer to hit its stride but from 1995 has been reassuringly consistent. The vintages from 2000 had greater purity of fruit, finesse, and length. Produced from a varying blend of 55 percent Cabernet Sauvignon, 34 percent Merlot, 10 percent Cabernet Franc, and 1 percent Petit Verdot, this is a generous wine, modern to a degree but with a finish that's pure, classic, minerally Graves.

Château Smith Haut Lafitte has been revived, the Cathiards proving that even great terroirs can benefit from a guiding hand.

Anne-Sophie Pic

Drôme Farmhouse Pigeon Roasted Whole in a Casserole

Ingredients
Serves 4

- 4 rhubarb stalks
- ¾ cup (150 g) superfine sugar
- 1 tablespoon grenadine syrup
- 2 very white celery stalks
- ⅔ cup (150 g) unsalted butter
- 2 ½ cups (500 ml) chicken stock or mineral water
- 3 ½ ounces (100 g) foie gras, cooked sous vide
- 2 pigeons
- 2 ⅛ cups (500 ml) brown stock (from powder or cube)
- Flat-leaf parsley
- Peanut oil
- Maldon sea salt and freshly ground Madagascar black pepper

The day before, make the candied rhubarb. Peel 2 rhubarb stalks. Place them on a perforated baking tray and sprinkle with ½ cup (100 g) of the sugar. Leave them to macerate overnight. The next day, remove the excess sugar and place the rhubarb in the refrigerator.

For the Rhubarb Juice. Rinse the other 2 rhubarb stalks and cut them into bars. Add ¼ cup (50 g) of sugar and 3 tablespoons of water. Cook in a bain-marie over low heat for about 2 hours. Strain and press the rhubarb gently to extract the maximum amount of juice. Add the grenadine syrup to the juice to obtain a wonderful color.

Lay the sugared bars of rhubarb in a small sauteuse pan, and pour in just enough rhubarb juice to cover them. Simmer on a low heat for 10 to 15 minutes, until the rhubarb is soft. Return the rhubarb to the refrigerator in its cooking juices.

Peel and wash the celery stalks. Cut into bars. In a sauteuse pan, sweat the celery in 1 ounce (30 g) of unsalted butter. Salt lightly. Cover the celery in the brown stock or water. Cook over low heat for 10 minutes. After cooking, let it cool in the stock.

Cut the cooked celery and rhubarb into pieces 2 inches (5 cm) long and ¼ inch (½ cm) thick. Cut the foie gras into bars the same size. Reserve the trimmings, which you will add to the stuffing.

Remove the thighs from each pigeon. Keep the pigeon breasts whole. Remove the livers and hearts. Keep them chilled to use in the stuffing. Completely bone the pigeon thighs and remove the meat without damaging the skin. Place in the refrigerator. Reserve the pigeon carcasses.

For the Stuffing. Cut the pigeon livers, hearts, and thigh meat into ¼-inch (½-cm) cubes. Mix the cubes together with a few bars of the foie gras and some chopped parsley. Season well. Stuff the pigeon thighs in the form of ballotines. Roast in the oven at 250° to 275°F (130 to 140°C) for about 1 hour and then keep chilled.

For the Pigeon Jus. Break up the pigeon carcasses. In a sauteuse pan, brown the pieces in 3 tablespoons (50 g) of butter and a little oil. When browned, spoon out any excess fat. Pour in enough brown stock to cover the carcasses. Simmer over low heat and then reduce by half. Strain and reserve the pigeon juices. Keep chilled.

Pan-fry the pigeon breasts skin-side down in 3 tablespoons (150 g) of butter and a little peanut oil until browned. Baste with the butter and then roast in the oven at 425°F (220°C) for about 5 minutes. Remove the pigeon from the oven and let rest for 5 minutes.

Heat up the pigeon thighs and breasts in 4 teaspoons (20 g) of butter over low heat. On dinner plates, layer the bars of celery, foie gras, and rhubarb. Add the chilled pigeon jus. Season with Maldon salt and freshly ground Madagascar pepper. Serve immediately.

Château Smith Haut Lafitte rouge 2001

This wine has an intensely deep red, fluid, and limpid appearance, with orange-red highlights. Its bouquet is pleasantly intense, with notes of red, crisp fruits, liquorice, and pepper and a harmonious, elegant woody undertone. With a smooth and round palate, the presence of spicy notes is immediately apparent and the finish is wonderfully satisfying. The tannins are supple, elegant, and pleasantly persistent. Serve at 64°F (18°C), decanted two hours before pouring.

—Denis Bertrand, Sommelier

The Châteaux

Château Haut-Brion

Cru Classé de Graves Red

Domaine Clarence Dillon

33608 Pessac Cedex, France

Tél. 33 (0)5 56 00 29 30

Fax 33 (0)5 56 98 75 14

info@haut-brion.com

www.haut-brion.com

Vineyard: A.O.C. Pessac-Léognan

Soil: gravelly soil with a clay-sand subsoil

Grape varieties: 43.9% Cabernet Sauvignon, 45.4% Merlot Noir, 9.7% Cabernet Franc, 1% Petit Verdot

Area under vines: 48.35 hectares

Average age of vines: 36 years

Pruning: double Guyot

Rootstock: 420A, 3309, Riparia

Vine density: 8,000–10,000 vines/hectare

Vinification: Harvesting: by hand; sorted on trailers

Temperature-controlled stainless steel tanks

Fermentation temperature: 86°F (30°C)

Aging in barrels: 18–22 months

Percentage of new barrels: 80%

Fining with egg whites

Production: 10,000–14,000 cases per year

Distribution: through the trade

Second wine: Château Bahans Haut-Brion; Le Clarence de Haut-Brion (from 2007 vintage on)

Owner: Domaine Clarence Dillon S.A.S.

President and Managing Director: H.R.H. Prince Robert of LUXEMBOURG

Estate Manager: Jean-Philippe DELMAS

Cellar Master and Oenologist: Jean-Philippe MASCLEF

Vineyard Manager: Pascal BARATIE

Château Bouscaut

Cru Classé de Graves Red and White

1477, avenue de Toulouse

33140 Cadaujac, France

Tél. 33 (0)5 57 83 12 20

Fax 33 (0)5 57 83 12 21

cb@chateau-bouscaut.com

www.chateau-bouscaut.com

Vineyard: A.O.C. Pessac-Léognan

Soil: gravel and clay on a calcareous base

Grape varieties, red: 55% Merlot, 40% Cabernet Sauvignon, 5% Malbec

Area under vines: 35 hectares

Grape varieties, white: 50% Sémillon, 50% Sauvignon

Area under vines: 7 hectares

Average age of vines: 37 years

Pruning: double and simple Guyot

Rootstock: Riparia, 3309, 101-14, 420A, Fercal

Vine density: 7,200 vines/hectare

Vinification: Harvesting: by hand, with small baskets and sorting tables before and after destemming

Red: Temperature-controlled stainless steel and cement tanks

Fermenting time: 15–30 days

Fermentation temperature: 75–82°F (24–28°C)

Aging in barrels: 16–18 months

Percentage of new barrels: 45%

Fining possible and adapted to each vintage

White: Fermented in barrels with regular bâtonnage

Fermentation temperature: 64–72°F (18–22°C)

Aging in barrels: 10–12 months

Percentage of new barrels: 45%

Production: Red: 8,000 cases per year

White: 2,000 cases per year

Sales: via Bordeaux wine merchants

Second wine: Les Chênes de Bouscaut

Owner: Sophie LURTON-COGOMBLES and Laurent COGOMBLES

Winemaker: Edouard MASSIE

Cellar Master: Patrice GRANDJEAN

Vineyard Manager: Manuel DA PAIXAO

Château Carbonnieux

Cru Classé de Graves Red and White

33850 Léognan, France

Tél. 33 (0)5 57 96 56 20

Fax 33 (0)5 57 96 59 19

info@chateau-carbonnieux.fr

www.carbonnieux.com

Vineyard: A.O.C. Pessac-Léognan

Soil: gravel, clay on a calcareous base

Grape varieties, red: 60% Cabernet Sauvignon, 30% Merlot, 7% Cabernet Franc, Petit Verdot, Carménère

Area under vines: 50 hectares

Grape varieties, white: 65% Sauvignon, 35% Sémillon

Area under vines: 42 hectares

Average age of vines: white 30 years; red 25 years

Pruning: double Guyot

Rootstock: 101-14, 3309, Riparia gloire, 420 A

Vine density: 7,200 vines/hectare

Vinification: Harvesting: by hand

Red: Temperature-controlled stainless steel tanks

Fermenting time: 21–28 days

Fermentation temperature: 86°F (30°C) max.

Aging in barrels: 16 months

Percentage of new barrels: 33%

Fining with egg whites

White: Fermented in barrels

Fermentation temperature: 68°F (20°C) max.

Aging in barrels: 10 months on the lees with bâtonnage

Percentage of new barrels: 25%

Filtering and fining with bentonite

Production: Red: 220,000 bottles

White: 130,000 bottles

Sales: via Bordeaux wine merchants

Second wine: Croix de Carbonnieux, Château Tour Léognan

Owner: SCEA A. Perrin et Fils

Managers: Eric and Philibert PERRIN

Consultant Oenologist: Denis DUBOURDIEU

Vineyard Manager: Jacky PICHON

Cellar Master: Romain RACHER

Domaine de Chevalier

Cru Classé de Graves Red and White

33850 Léognan, France

Tél. 33 (0)5 56 64 16 16

Fax 33 (0)5 56 64 18 18

olivierbernard@domainedechevalier.com

www.domainedechevalier.com

Vineyard: A.O.C. Pessac-Léognan

Soil: gravel on a well-drained clay-gravel subsoil

Grape varieties, red: 65% Cabernet Sauvignon, 30% Merlot, 3% Petit Verdot, 2% Cabernet Franc

Area under vines: 41 hectares

Grape varieties, white: 70% Sauvignon, 30% Sémillon

Area under vines: 6 hectares

Average age of vines: 25 years

Pruning: double Guyot

Rootstock: 101-14, 420A, 3309, Riparia

Vine density: 10,000 vines/hectare

Vinification: Harvesting: by hand, with small crates

Red: Temperature-controlled stainless steel tanks

Fermenting time: 3 weeks

Aging in barrels: 16–20 months

Percentage of new barrels: 50%

White: 3-5 successive sortings

Aging in barrels: 18 months with bâtonnage

Percentage of new barrels: 35%

Production: Red: 120,000 bottles

White: 18,000 bottles

Sales: via Bordeaux wine merchants

Second wine: L'Esprit de Chevalier

Owner: The BERNARD Family

Société Civile du Domaine de Chevalier

Managing Director: Olivier BERNARD

Assistant Manager: Rémi EDANGE

Technical Manager: Thomas STONESTREET

Consulting Oenologists: Denis DUBOURDIEU, Stéphane DERENONCOURT

Château Couhins

Cru Classé de Graves White

INRA – Château Couhins

Chemin de la Gravette, BP 81

33883 Villenave d'Ornon Cedex, France

Tél. 33 (0)5 56 30 77 61

Fax 33 (0)5 56 30 70 49

couhins@bordeaux.inra.fr

www.chateau-couhins.fr

Vineyard: A.O.C. Pessac-Léognan

Soil: deep gravel and clayey-chalky slopes, clayey subsoil

Grape varieties, white: 90% Sauvignon, 10% Sémillon

Area under vines: 6 hectares

Grape varieties, red: 50% Merlot, 40% Cabernet Sauvignon, 8% Cabernet Franc, 2% Petit Verdot

Area under vines: 17 hectares

Average age of vines: 25 years

Pruning: double Guyot and Cordon

Vinification: Harvest: by hand, using small crates; sorting in vineyard and cellar stainless steel tanks

Aging in barrels and tanks

Production: White: 20,000 bottles

Sales: via Bordeaux wine merchants

Other production: Château Couhins (red); Couhins La Gravette (red and white); La Dame de Couhins (red)

Owner: INRA

Manager: Dominique FORGET

Contact: Clément BOURIEZ

Consultant Oenologists: Denis DUBOURDIEU, Valérie LAVIGNE-CRUEGE

Château Couhins-Lurton

Cru Classé de Graves White

48, chemin de Martillac
33140 Villenave d'Ornon, France
Tél. 33 (0)5 57 25 58 58
Fax 33 (0)5 57 74 98 59
andrelurton@andrelurton.com
www.andrelurton.com

Vineyard: A.O.C. Pessac-Léognan
Soil: gravel and sandy gravel
Grape variety: 100% Sauvignon
Area under vines: 5.5 hectares
Average age of vines: 18 years
Pruning: single Guyot
Rootstock: 101-14
Vine density: 6,500–8,500 vines/hectare
Vinification: Harvesting: by hand, with small crates and sorting
Temperature-controlled stainless steel tanks
Fermentation in barrels
Fermentation temperature: 64°F (18°C)
Aging in barrels: 10 months
Percentage of new barrels: 50%
Filtering and fining
Production: 2,750 cases per year
Commercialisation: France, USA, Canada, Netherlands, Belgium, Germany
Owner: André LURTON
Consultant Oenologist: Denis DUBOURDIEU
Oenologist: M. GAILLARD and V. CRUEGE

Château de Fieuzal

Cru Classé de Graves Red

124, avenue de Mont-de-Marsan
33850 Léognan, France
Tél. 33 (0)5 56 64 77 86
Fax 33 (0)5 56 64 18 88
infochato@fieuzal.com
www.fieuzal.com

Vineyard: A.O.C. Pessac-Léognan
Soil: gravelly sand
Grape varieties, red: 65% Cabernet Sauvignon, 25% Merlot, 6% Cabernet Franc,
4% Petit Verdot
Area under vines: 65 hectares
Grape varieties, white: 70% Sauvignon, 30% Sémillon
Area under vines: 10 hectares
Vinification: Harvesting: by hand, grapes sorted before gathering
Temperature-controlled stainless steel tanks
Fermenting time: 20–30 days
Aging in barrels: 12–18 months
Percentage of new barrels: 50%
Production: 13,000 cases per year
Château de Fieuzal red: 10,000 cases
Château de Fieuzal white: 2,000 cases
Sales: via Bordeaux wine merchants
Second wine: L'Abeille de Fieuzal
Owner: Brenda and Lochlann QUINN
Manager: Stephen CARRIER
Consultant: Hubert de BOUARD

Château Haut-Bailly

Cru Classé de Graves Red

33850 Léognan, France
Tél. 33 (0)5 56 64 75 11
Fax 33 (0)5 56 64 53 60
mail@chateau-haut-bailly.com
www.chateau-haut-bailly.com

Vineyard: A.O.C. Pessac-Léognan
Soil: sand and gravel
Grape varieties: 64% Cabernet Sauvignon, 30% Merlot, 6% Cabernet Franc
Area under vines: 30 hectares
Average age of vines: 35 years
Pruning: double Guyot
Rootstock: 101-14, 420A, 3309, Riparia gloire
Vine density: 10,000 vines/hectare
Vinification: Harvesting: by hand with double sorting
Temperature-controlled stainless steel and cement tanks
Fermentation time: 3 weeks
Fermentation temperature: 86°F (30°C)
Aging in barrels: 16 months
Percentage of new barrels: 50%
Fining with egg whites
Production: 10,000 cases per year
Marketing: via Bordeaux wine merchants

Château La Mission Haut-Brion

Cru Classé de Graves Red

Domaine Clarence Dillon
33608 Pessac Cedex, France
Tél. 33 (0)5 56 00 29 30
Fax 33 (0)5 56 98 75 14
info@haut-brion.com
www.mission-haut-brion.com

Vineyard: A.O.C. Pessac-Léognan
Soil: gravelly soil with a clay-sand subsoil
Grape varieties: 47% Cabernet Sauvignon, 42.7% Merlot Noir, 10.3% Cabernet Franc
Area under vines: 26.6 hectares
Average age of vines: 27 years
Pruning: double Guyot
Rootstock: 420A, 3309, 101-14, Riparia
Vine density: 10,000 vines/hectare
Vinification: Harvesting: by hand; sorted on trailers
Stainless steel tanks
Fermentation temperature: 86°F (30°C)
Aging in barrels: 18–22 months
Percentage of new barrels: 80%
Fining with egg whites
Production: 6,000–7,000 cases per year
Sales: via Bordeaux wine merchants
Second wine: La Chapelle de la Mission Haut-Brion
Owner: Domaine Clarence Dillon S.A.S.
President and Managing Director:
H.R.H. Prince Robert of LUXEMBOURG
Estate Manager: Jean-Philippe DELMAS
Cellar Master and Oenologist:
Jean-Philippe MASCLEF
Vineyard Manager: Pascal BARATIE
Second wine: La Parde de Haut-Bailly
Owner: Robert G. WILMERS
Managing Director: Véronique SANDERS
Technical Director: Gabriel VIALARD
Consulting Oenologists: Pascal
RIBEREAU-GAYON, Denis DUBOURDIEU,
Jean-Bernard DELMAS

Château La Tour Haut-Brion

Cru Classé de Graves Red

Domaine Clarence Dillon
33608 Pessac Cedex, France
Tél. 33 (0)5 56 00 29 30
Fax 33 (0)5 56 98 75 14
info@haut-brion.com
www.la-tour-haut-brion.com

Vineyard: A.O.C. Pessac-Léognan
Soil: gravelly soil with a clay-sand subsoil
Grape varieties: 44.3% Cabernet Sauvignon, 34% Merlot Noir, 21.7% Cabernet Franc
Area under vines: 5 hectares
Average age of vines: 15 years
Pruning: double Guyot
Rootstock: 420A, 3309
Vine density: 10,000 vines/hectare
Vinification: Harvesting: by hand; sorted on trailers
Stainless steel tanks
Fermentation temperature: 86°F (30°C)
Aging in barrels: 18–22 months
Percentage of new barrels: 30%
Fining with egg whites
Production: 2,000–2,500 cases per year
Sales: via Bordeaux wine merchants
Owner: Domaine Clarence Dillon S.A.S.
President and Managing Director:
H.R.H. Prince Robert of LUXEMBOURG
Estate Manager: Jean-Philippe DELMAS
Cellar Master and Oenologist:
Jean-Philippe MASCLEF
Vineyard Manager: Pascal BARATIE

Château Latour-Martillac

Cru Classé de Graves Red and White

SCEA Vignobles Jean Kressmann
33650 Martillac, France
Tél. 33 (0)557 97 71 11
Fax 33 (0)557 97 71 17
latourmartillac@svjk.com
www.latourmartillac.com

Vineyard: A.O.C. Pessac-Léognan
Soil: Pyrenean gravel on terraces
Grape varieties, red: 60% Cabernet Sauvignon, 35% Merlot, 5% Petit Verdot
Area under vines: 36 hectares
Grape varieties, white: 55% Sémillon, 40% Sauvignon Blanc, 5% Muscadelle
Area under vines: 10 hectares
Average age of vines: 35 years
Pruning: double Guyot
Rootstock: 101-14, 3309
Vine density: 7,200–8,500 vines/hectare
Vinification: Harvesting: by hand
Red: Temperature-controlled stainless steel and wooden tanks
Fermenting time: 3–4 weeks
Aging in barrels: 14–16 months
Percentage of new barrels: 35–50%
White: Fermentation in wooden barrels
Aging in barrels: 10–15 months on the lees
Percentage of new barrels: 35%
Production: Red: 12,500 cases per year
White: 3,000 cases per year
Sales: via Bordeaux wine merchants
Second wine: Lagrave-Martillac
Owner: GFA Latour-Martillac
Managers: Tristan and Loïc KRESSMANN
Oenologist: Valérie VIALARD
Vineyard Manager: Denis WENDLING

Château Laville Haut-Brion

Cru Classé de Graves White

Domaine Clarence Dillon
33608 Pessac Cedex, France
Tél. 33 (0)5 56 00 29 30
Fax 33 (0)5 56 98 75 14
info@haut-brion.com
www.laville-haut-brion.com

Vineyard: A.O.C. Pessac-Léognan
Soil: gravelly soil with a clay-sand subsoil
Grape varieties: 87.9% Sémillon, 12.1% Sauvignon
Area under vines: 2.55 hectares
Average age of vines: 63 years
Pruning: double Guyot
Rootstock: 420A, 3309
Vine density: 10,000 vines/hectare
Vinification: Harvesting: by hand, with small crates
Fermentation temperature: 68°F (20°C)
Aging in barrels: 9–12 months
Percentage of new barrels: 50%
Fining with egg whites
Production: 650–850 cases per year
Sales: via Bordeaux wine merchants
Owner: Domaine Clarence Dillon S.A.S.
President and Managing Director:
H.R.H. Prince Robert of LUXEMBOURG
Estate Manager: Jean-Philippe DELMAS
Cellar Master and Oenologist:
Jean-Philippe MASCLEF
Vineyard Manager: Pascal BARATIE

Château Malartic-Lagravière

Cru Classé de Graves Red and White

43, avenue de Mont-de-Marsan
33850 Léognan, France
Tél. 33 (0)5 56 64 75 08
Fax 33 (0)5 56 64 99 66
malartic-lagraviere@malartic-lagraviere.com
www.malartic-lagraviere.com

Vineyard: A.O.C. Pessac-Léognan
Soil: well-drained gravel and clay gravel on shelly limestone and clay subsoil
Grape varieties, red: 45% Cabernet Sauvignon, 45% Merlot, 8% Cabernet Franc, 2% Petit Verdot
Area under vines: 46 hectares
Grape varieties, white: 80% Sauvignon, 20% Sémillon
Area under vines: 7 hectares
Average age of vines: 25 years
Pruning: double Guyot
Vine density: 10,000 vines/hectare
Vinification: Red: Harvesting: by hand, with double sorting
Temperature-controlled stainless steel and wooden tanks
Fermenting time: 3–5 weeks
Aging in barrels: 15–22 months
Percentage of new barrels: 50–70%
White: Harvesting: by hand, with successive sorting
Fermentation in barrels
Fermenting time: 3–5 weeks
Aging in barrels: 10–15 months
Percentage of new barrels: 40–60%

Production: Red: 17,000 cases per year
White: 2,500 cases per year
Sales: via Bordeaux wine merchants
Second wine: La Réserve de Malartic,
Le Sillage de Malartic
Owner: Alfred-Alexandre BONNIE
General Manager: Jean-Jacques BONNIE
Winemaker/Oenologist: Philippe GARCIA
Vineyard Manager: Benoît PREVOTEAU
Consultant Oenologists: Michel ROLLAND,
Athanase FAKORELLIS

Château Olivier

Cru Classé de Graves Red and White

175, avenue de Bordeaux
33850 Léognan, France
Tél. 33 (0)5 56 64 73 31
Fax 33 (0)5 56 64 54 23
mail@chateau-olivier.com
www.chateau-olivier.com

Vineyard: A.O.C. Pessac-Léognan
Soil: 12 different types of soil
including compact gravel, deep gravel,
gravel on marl, marl, and Miocene limestone
Grape varieties, red: Cabernet Sauvignon,
Merlot, Cabernet Franc
Area under vines: 45 hectares
Grape varieties, white: Sauvignon,
Sémillon, Muscadelle
Area under vines: 10 hectares
Average age of vines: 30 years
Pruning: double Guyot
Rootstock: 101-14, Riparia, 3309
Vine density: 8,000 vines/hectare
Vinification: Harvesting: by hand, with small
crates; sorted in vineyard and winery
Red: Temperature-controlled stainless
steel tanks
Fermenting time: 3 weeks
Aging in barrels: 12 months
Percentage of new barrels: 33%
White: Fermenting in barrels
Filtering and fining with egg whites
White: Fermenting in barrels
Aging in barrels: 10 months
Percentage of new barrels: 33%
Production: Red: 10,000 cases per year
White: 3,000 cases per year
Sales: via Bordeaux wine merchants
Second wine: La Seigneurerie d'Olivier,
Le Dauphin d'Olivier

Owner: Jean-Jacques DE BETHMANN
General Manager: Laurent LEBRUN
Winemaker: Damien BIELLE
Vineyard Manager: Vincent FINDELING

Château Pape Clément

Cru Classé de Graves Red

216, avenue du Docteur Nancel Pénard
33600 Pessac, France
Tél. 33 (0)5 57 26 38 38
Fax 33 (0)5 57 26 38 39
chateau@pape-clement.com
www.pape-clement.com

Vineyard: A.O.C. Pessac-Léognan
Soil: Pyrenean gravel
Grape varieties, red: 54% Cabernet Sauvignon,
43% Merlot, 3% Petit Verdot
Area under vines: 30 hectares
Grape varieties, white: 40% Sauvignon Blanc,
35% Sémillon, 16% Sauvignon Gris,
9% Muscadelle
Area under vines: 3 hectares
Average age of vines: 31 years
Pruning: Bordelaise
Vine density: 7,700 vines/hectare
Vinification: Harvesting: by hand
Temperature-controlled wooden tanks
Fermenting time: 30-40 days
Fermentation temperature: 82°F (28°C)
Aging in barrels: 18–22 months
Percentage of new barrels: 100%
Production: 90,000 bottles
Sales : via Bordeaux wine merchants
Other production: Château Pape Clément white
Second wine: Clémentin du Château Pape
Clément
Owner: Bernard MAGREZ
Technical Manager: Patrice HATEAU
Cellar Masters: Jean-Charles FOURNIE,
Gilles PAQUEREAU

Château Smith Haut Lafitte

Cru Classé de Graves Red

33650 Martillac, France
Tél. 33 (0)5 57 83 11 22
Fax 33 (0)5 57 83 11 21
f.cathiard@smith-haut-lafitte.com
www.smith-haut-lafitte.com

Vineyard: A.O.C. Pessac-Léognan
Soil: Günzian gravel
Grape varieties, red: 59% Cabernet Sauvignon,
30% Merlot, 10% Cabernet Franc,
1% Petit Verdot
Area under vines: 56 hectares
Grape varieties, white: 90% Sauvignon Blanc,
5% Sauvignon Gris, 5% Sémillon
Area under vines: 11 hectares
Average age of vines: 38 years
Pruning: Bordelaise
Rootstock: Riparia, 101-14, 3309C
Vine density: 7,500–9,000 vines/hectare
Vinification: Harvesting: by hand,
with small crates
Temperature-controlled wooden tanks
Fermenting time: 28–38 days
Fermentation temperature: 82–86°F (28–30°C)
Aging in barrels and vats: 18 months,
on the lees with bâtonnage
Percentage of new barrels: 70%
Production: 10,000 cases per year
Sales: via Bordeaux wine merchants
Second wine: Les Hauts de Smith (red and white)
Owner: Daniel et Florence CATHIARD
Technical Director: Fabien TEITGEN

The Chefs

01. Georges Blanc
Relais & Châteaux Georges Blanc
01540 Vonnas, France
www.georgesblanc.com

02. Daniel Boulud
Restaurant Daniel
60 East 65th Street
New York, NY 10065
www.danielnyc.com

03. Anne-Sophie Pic
Maison Pic
Restaurant Gastronomique
285, avenue Victor-Hugo
26000 Valence, France
www.pic-valence.fr

04. Régis Marcon
Restaurant Régis & Jacques Marcon
Larsiallas
43290 St-Bonnet-le-Froid, France
www.regismarcon.fr

05. Christopher Coutanceau
Restaurant Christopher Coutanceau
Plage de la Concurrence
17000 La Rochelle, France
www.coutanceaularochelle.com

06. Michel Trama
Les Loges de l'Aubergade
52, rue royale
47270 Puymirol, France
www.aubergade.com

07. Pierre Gagnaire
Restaurant Pierre Gagnaire
6, rue Balzac
75008 Paris, France
www.pierregagnaire.com

08. Peter Goossens
Restaurant Hof van Cleve
Riemegemstraat 1
9770 Kruishoutem, Belgium
www.hofvancleve.com

09. Jacques & Laurent Pourcel
Le Jardin des Sens
11, avenue Saint-Lazare
34000 Montpellier, France
www.jardindessens.com

10. Éric Ripert
Le Bernardin
787 Seventh Avenue
New York, NY 10019
www.le-bernardin.com

11. Patrick Guilbaud
Restaurant Patrick Guilbaud
21 Merrion Street Upper
Dublin 2, Ireland
www.restaurantpatrickguilbaud.ie

12. Michel Guérard
Restaurant Les Prés d'Eugénie
40320 Eugénie-les-Bains, France
www.michelguerard.com

13. Éric Briffard
Restaurant le V
Four Seasons Hotel Georges V
31, avenue Georges V
75008 Paris, France
www.fourseasons.com/paris

14. Alain Passard
Restaurant L'Arpège
84, rue de Varenne
75007 Paris, France
www.alain-passard.com

Photos : 01 © Isabelle Rozenbaum. 02 © Medilek.
03 © Jeff Nalin. 09 © Olivier Maynard. 10 © Brigitte Lacombe.
14 © Virginie Klecka.

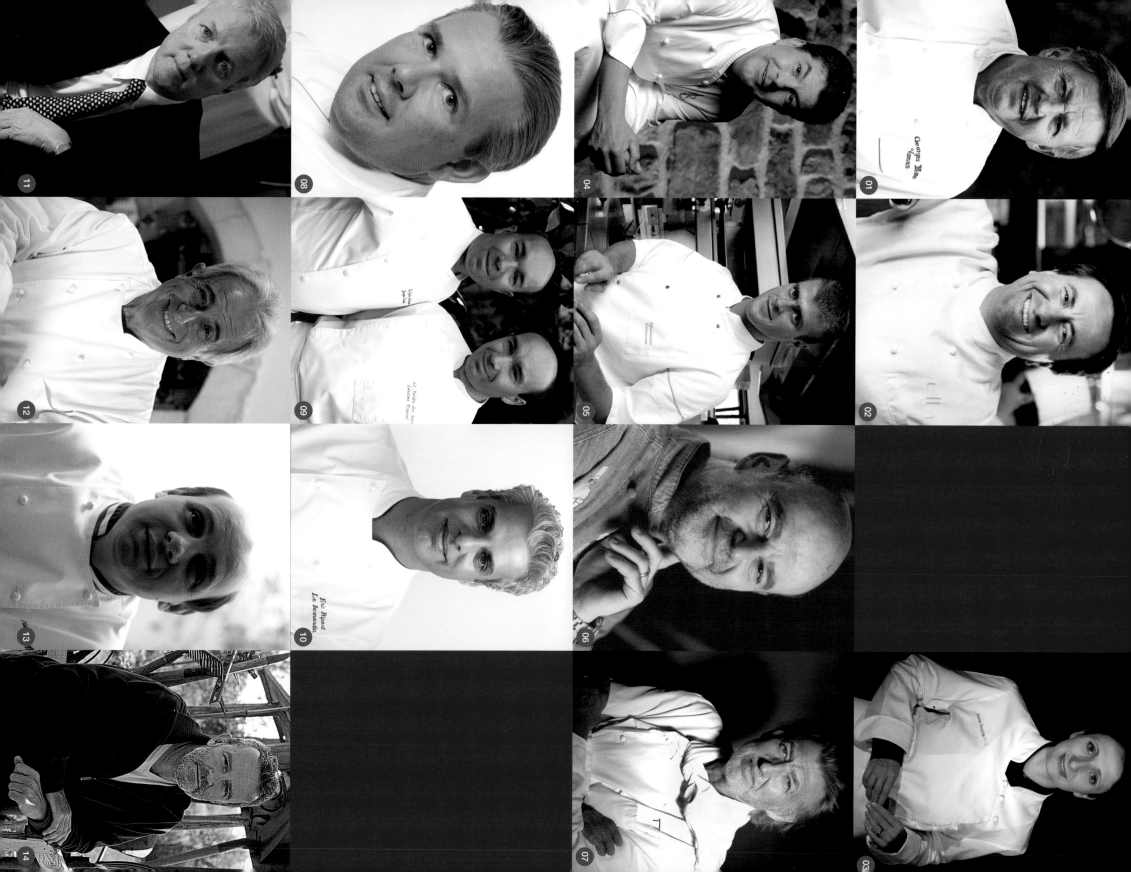

Acknowledgments

The Heart of Bordeaux arose from a desire to dedicate a few pages to the quintessence of sixteen *crus*, their fascinating histories, their admirable men and women, and their elegant wines.

This book owes a great deal to its authors—Michel Bettane, Hugh Johnson, and James Lawther— faithful ambassadors of the *Crus Classés* of Graves around the world;

the extraordinary participation of Michelin-starred Chefs and their Sommeliers;

photographer Alain Benoit, for his keen eye,

and last but not least Éditions de La Martinière, for orchestrating the project so perfectly.

Alain Benoit would like to thank the following for their precious help
the team at Studio DEEPIX in Bordeaux,
and the teams at every Château for their support and active contribution out in the field.

www.crus-classes-de-graves.com

www.theheartofbordeaux.com

Published in 2009 by Stewart, Tabori & Chang

An imprint of ABRAMS

Copyright © 2008 by La Martinière, an imprint of La Martinière Groupe, Paris

All rights reserved. No portion of this book may be reproduced, stored in a retrieval system, or transmitted in any form or by any means, mechanical, electronic, photocopying, recording, or otherwise, without written permission from the publisher.

Library of Congress Cataloging-in-Publication DataLawther, James.
The heart of Bordeaux: the greatest wines from Graves Châteaux / by James Lawther;
photography, Alain Benoit; preface, Hugh Johnson; introduction, Michel Bettane.

ISBN 978-1-58479-814-9
1. Wine and wine making--France--Bordeaux.
2. Vineyards--France--Bordeaux.
1. Title.
TP553.L327 2009
641.2'209447144--dc22
2009011627

La Martinière Edition

Coordinating editor: Claire Arjakovsky and Nathalie Mayevski
Recipe editor: Virginie Mahieux
Copyeditor: Renaud Bezombes
Graphic design and production: Christian Kirk-Jensen/Danish Pastry Design
Preface, Introduction, and Recipes translation, English-language edition: I.D.O. Paris21

STC Edition

Project manager: Magali Veillon
Recipe editor: Leah Stewart

The text of this book was composed in Berkeley Book and Clearface Regular.
Printed and bound in France
10 9 8 7 6 5 4 3 2 1

ABRAMS
THE ART OF BOOKS SINCE 1949

115 West 18th Street
New York, NY 10011
www.abramsbooks.com